Shiksa Speaks: A White, Non-Jew's Understanding of the Cuban Jewish Diaspora and Its Legacy

PEACE EDUCATION

SERIES EDITORS:
Laura Finley, Barry University in Miami Shores
Robin Cooper, Nova Southeastern University

Series Description

In our times, peace education efforts can be positive, integrative, restorative, generative, and transformative. In other words, rather than defining peace education in the negative such as education for the elimination of violence, peace education efforts can be understood in the positive as creative, generative efforts that integrate knowledge and action, that integrate differences in ways that both honor diversity and establish common ground. Peace education works on bringing people together. This series on peace education hopes to illuminate the problems, challenges, and rewards associated with using educational means to diminish/ eliminate and avoid conflicts. How effective is peace education in bringing about peace? What are its strengths and weaknesses as a strategy to achieve peace? How is peace education carried out in different venuesâ€"colleges, schools, and community groups? How is peace taught in different cultures? The editors welcome manuscripts about war and peace and other peace studies themes that exhibit a clear connection to teaching and learning for solutions to promoting harmony and to building a peaceful world.

Published Titles

Teaching Peace Through Popular Culture, 2nd Edition by Laura L. Finley

Coronavirus and Vulnerable People: Addressing the Divide in Harm and Responses and Exploring Implications for a More Peaceful World by Laura L. Finley & Pamela D. Hall

Lessons for Creating a Culture of Character and Peace in Your Classroom: A Playbook for Teachers by Edward F. DeRoche, , C. J. Moloney, & Patricia J. McGinty

The New Peace Linguistics and the Role of Language in Conflict by Andy Curtis

Humanities Perspectives in Peace Education: Re-Engaging the Heart of Peace Studies by Nicole L. Johnson

Peace is Everyone's Business by Lowell Ewert & Frederick Bird

Experiential Learning in Higher Education: Issues, Ideas, and Challenges for Promoting Peace and Justice by Laura L. Finley & Glenn A. Bowen

Shiksa Speaks: A White, Non-Jew's Understanding of the Cuban Jewish Diaspora and Its Legacy

LAURA FINLEY

Barry University, Miami Shores, Florida

emerald
PUBLISHING

United Kingdom – North America – Japan – India – Malaysia – China

Emerald Publishing Limited
Emerald Publishing, Floor 5, Northspring, 21-23 Wellington Street, Leeds LS1 4DL

First edition 2025

Editorial matter and selection © 2025 Laura Finley

Published under exclusive licence by Emerald Publishing Limited.
Reprints and permissions service

Contact: www.copyright.com

British Library Cataloguing in Publication Data

A catalogue record for this book is available from the British Library

ISBN: 978-1-83708-494-4 (hardcover)
ISBN: 978-1-83708-495-1 (paperback)
ISBN: 978-1-83708-496-8 (electronic PDF)

CONTENTS

FOREWORD

Heidi Heft LaPorte

In her compelling work, Dr. Laura Finley, a distinguished Professor of Sociology & Criminology at Barry University, encourages readers to explore the intriguing depths of the history of Cuban immigration to the United States. With candidness, she offers hner unique perspective as a 'shiksa,' a non-Jewish woman who, as both a family member and an outsider, brings forth a distinctive lens through which to view the journey of Jewish immigrants. This journey takes them from the tumultuous landscapes of Eastern Europe to the vibrant heart of Cuba and, ultimately, the United States. Dr. Finley's exploration explores the emotional terrain of the human experience, where resilience intertwines with cultural identity. Through her work, she vividly portrays immigrants' struggles, triumphs, contradictions, and the unspoken dreams that permeated their lives.

As we navigate these pages, Dr. Finley confronts us with the complexities of refuge, identity, and immigration, all while maintaining the mindful perspective of an observer who is profoundly empathetic yet inherently distinct from the cultural narrative she describes. She highlights the pivotal role of the Cuban Revolution and how the 'Jewban' identity symbolizes a unique cultural amalgamation, epitomizing adaptation, resilience, and the longing for belonging. The narrative reaches into the heart of the Cuban Jewish community, exploring the nuanced dy-

Shiksa Speaks: A White, Non-Jew's Understanding of the
Cuban Jewish Diaspora and Its Legacy, vii–viii.
Copyright © 2025 *Laura Finley*
Published under exclusive licence by Emerald Publishing Limited
HB: 978-1-83708-494-4, PB: 978-1-83708-495-1, ePDF: 978-1-83708-496-8

namics of their identities, professional achievements, and the distinctive 'Cuban privilege' that has shaped their exile experience.

While Dr. Finley's narrative is a rich and empathetic exploration of the 'Jewban' experience, it is essential to recognize the broader academic discourse surrounding topics of identity and immigration. Dr. Finley's work situates itself within these complex conversations, offering a deep dive into the Jewish-Cuban narrative and acknowledging the myriad ways it intersects with and diverges from other immigrant experiences.

Dr. Finley addresses the delicate subject of privilege and the Cuban community's intricate relationship with other groups in this narrative. With tact and sensitivity, she, as an outsider, sheds light on the contrasts and tensions that arise when disparate experiences of marginalization and resilience intersect. This book does not shy away from these tough conversations; instead, it approaches them thoughtfully, encouraging readers to reflect on the broader implications of social justice and our collective responsibility towards inclusivity.

By framing the 'Jewban' experience within the broader context of global immigration and cultural integration from her unique vantage point, Dr. Finley's work contributes to a crucial and ongoing conversation. It is a testament to her commitment to narrating history and engaging critically with it, prompting readers to reflect not only on the resilience and triumphs of the Cuban Jewish community but also on our collective understanding of identity, belonging, and the dynamic landscapes of cultural heritage.

Dr. Finley's exploration is not just an invitation to reflect—it's a call to action. It urges us to approach these stories with empathy, understanding, and a commitment to thoughtfully engage with the intricate mosaic of our shared human experience. This book challenges us to use our voices and privilege to foster equity and inclusivity, promoting a synergy of compassion and innovation.

As we embark on this journey with Dr. Finley, we are reminded that the stories we tell and the histories we narrate are not just recollections of the past but active participants in shaping our future. As we turn each page, we honor not just the collective narrative but also the individual stories that form the mosaic of our history.

With hope for a world of deeper understanding and shared stories,

—Dr. Heidi Heft LaPorte
Associate Professor,
Barry University School of Social Work

INTRODUCTION

I am Shiksa. In Yiddish that is a term—sometimes a disparaging one—for a gentile or non-religious women. Until a few years ago, at the time 45 years old, I had no idea what that meant. I am White, of nearly 100 percent British, Scottish and Irish origin, and was raised in rural Michigan. I grew up knowing absolutely no Jewish people. If they lived in my broader community, I was unaware of them. I am also *Blanca no Judia*, Spanish for White-non-Jew. In fact, I am not religious at all. Yet here I am, writing a book about Cuban Jews. How did that happen, one might wonder? As sad as it is to admit, growing up I had no idea that there were Jewish people in the Caribbean and Latin America, and that some of them emigrated to the U.S. I knew next to nothing about Latin American history, and specifically, Cuban history, which has become such an important part of my life. In my rural Michigan school, we were taught about the Bay of Pigs and the Cuban Missile Crisis, and that Castro was the communist devil. That is all. I am not proud of that lack of knowledge, but rural Michigan educators simply did not prioritize teaching about Latin America at all, at least not when I was in school.

Then I moved to South Florida in 2005. South Florida is a treasure trove of diversity, and here I have met, worked with, and befriended people from all over and from many religious groups. But even more, I met Cuban Jews, Jewbans, as they are called. Although far from fluent, I have brushed up on my Spanish (last

Shiksa Speaks: A White, Non-Jew's Understanding of the
Cuban Jewish Diaspora and Its Legacy, ix–xv.
Copyright © 2025 *Laura Finley*
Published under exclusive licence by Emerald Publishing Limited
HB: 978-1-83708-494-4, PB: 978-1-83708-495-1, ePDF: 978-1-83708-496-8

studied formally in high school in 1989). In 2018. I even started dating a Jewban, and learned about and became some part of his large and close extended family as we subsequently married in 2020. The family is wonderful—welcoming, loving, and all quite successful. My in-laws were both born in Cuba to families that emigrated from Eastern Europe. All left due to intolerance and lack of economic opportunity in the 1920s and had intended to make a new life in the US. When the US significantly changed immigration laws in 1924, however, many Jews in their situation ended up staying in Cuba. They described a lovely, vibrant island with Jewish family and friends living and working near to one another. Until the revolution in 1959 that resulted in Fulgencio Batista fleeing the island and Fidel Castro taking power. My in-laws married and left for the US, never to return. In the next few years, all of their family also emigrated to the US and established themselves anew, once more.

When my husband's father passed away in 2021, in part due to blood cancer and in part due to COVID-19, I sat with the family as they mourned. Everyone shared stories, and I learned even more about the Jewbans and their double diaspora from Eastern Europe to Cuba then to the US. At one point my husband said, "Someone should write a book about our family." I have written a lot of scholarly, reference work but never this kind of thing, however, I declared, "I write sometimes, maybe I could?" Hence was cooked up a proposal, thankfully which was granted by my employer, Barry University, for sabbatical in Spring 2023 to conduct in-depth interviews with his extended family and others they may connect me to so as to better understand the Cuban Jewish double diaspora and how it has affected later generations. This work, whatever it may be, is a tribute to Jack Bekerman, who I was lucky to know for a brief time.

I have learned a great deal and am grateful for the opportunity provided by the family and other connections as well as by my university. I am also grateful to have been able to visit Cuba for three days in July 2023. My husband and daughter joined me, and not only did we see most of the important landmarks in Havana, but we were also able to tour Jewish Havana. We visited the Patronato, where my in-laws were married, visited the oldest Jewish cemetery, and walked around the Jewish area of old town. It was eye opening, and I have included in this book some observations and experiences from the trip.

Despite all that I have learned, I remain interested in learning more. The Jewbans are amongst the most welcoming and interesting people I have met (I think that is accurate, even if I am biased from being part of the family). They also have some fascinating family narratives that I think can add to the scholarly research on immigration, diaspora, and resilience. I am proud to share what I can. Throughout the book I have woven in memories, ideas, and quotes from those I interviewed, information acquired through reviewing documents the family retained, as well as additional research I conducted from scholarly texts. I make no claim that my review of the research is exhaustive, although I did my best to acquire as much background knowledge as I could. Importantly, as a participant researcher, I recognize that the memories shared with me may have been influenced by my relationship with the interviewees. That is a limitation of participatory research, but I believe the benefits in this case were tremendous, as it can help understand the role that family narratives shape in diasporic communities. Further, as LaPorte et al. (2009) noted, "In general, commentators caution that personal testimonies about life in Cuba, on which much of the literature is based, are very emotionally charged and may be subject to subtle manipulation—deliberate or not—to promote a particular worldview" (p. 315).

My interview research included interviews with a total of 22 individuals—all but one is somehow related to the family. One is an old friend from Cuba who lives in South Florida and has remained close. Each interview was a minimum of 30 minutes in length, with several lasting multiple hours. All interviewees gave their permission to use their names and to quote them as needed. A profile of the interviewees is provided below.

NOTE: I have found various spellings for some of the family members from Eastern Europe. Throughout the book I used consistently the spelling I saw most frequently.

EXILE GENERATION

Lilia is almost 80 and left Cuba immediately after marrying Jack, who passed away in 2021. She was 16 when she left the island, and he was 23. She is my mother-in-law.

Ester is Lilia's cousin on her mother, Consuelo's, side. She is a professor emeritus who is the only family member to have extensively studied the Jewban experience and has been to Cuba several times. She was 6 when she left the island.

Rachel S. is Ester's sister, also Lilia's cousin on her mother's side. She is a social worker and, being not yet 4 when the family left the island, has more impression of it than distinct memories.

Enrique/Henry is Jack's brother. He is ten years younger so is in his mid-1970s. He and his family left Cuba after the Bay of Pigs invasion. He was a teenager and has quite distinct memories of living in Havana and the passage to the US.

Anita was married to Lilia's brother, Leo. She was actually born in the US because her parents decided she would have a better life if she had American citizenship from the outset. They moved to Cuba when she was a baby, then to the US as part of the exile generation. Gregg and Jeff are her children with Leo (as is Eric, but he was not involved in the research).

Marcos is different than the other exiles in that he was sent by his family to Los Angeles as part of Operation Pedro Pan, an initiative that sent some 14,000 unaccompanied children ages 6–18 to the US between 1960 and 1962. Approximately 400 Cuban Jewish children were included. He is a professor at Florida International University and Barry University and is still close with his childhood friend, Enrique.

xii • SHIKSA SPEAKS

Raquel is Lilia's daughter Lisette's mother-in-law. She came to the US as an exile but her husband, Jose (known as Pepe) could not join her because he was in a labor camp trying to unlawfully leave the country. Pepe arrived in 1963. He was Sephardic, and their relationship was one of the rare intermarriages of Ashkenazi and Sephardic in Cuba. Pepe passed away in 2017.

SECOND GENERATION

David, my husband. is Lilia's middle child and is 57. He was born in New York and moved with his family to Miami when he was 10. Davis is the most interested in the family history of anyone in his immediate family, likely due to the fact that he grew up hearing stories from his maternal and paternal grandmothers about their lives in Eastern Europe and then Cuba.

Perry is Lilia's oldest son. He was also born in New York but has lived in South Florida since he was a teenager. He also has memories of his grandmothers and his grandfather on his mother's side.

Jodi is Perry's wife. Her family is not Cuban but having been with Perry and the family for more than 30 years, she offered valuable insight on the stories that have been passed down.

Lisette is Lilia's youngest child. She barely remembers their time in New York, as she was just 5 when the family moved to Miami. She admits she is not very "political," nor has she had that much interest in the family history but is proud to be Jewban.

Alan is Lisette's husband. His mother is Raquel, and his father was Pepe. He did not meet his father for several years due to his imprisonment in Cuba.

Jeff is David and Lisette's cousin, son of Lilia's brother Leon. Born in Miami, he is one of the few who left the geographic vicinity of his family, never to return.

Gregg is Jeff's brother, another cousin of David and Lisette. He, too, was born in Miami but left as an adult and has not returned to live near the family. He maintains a significant interest in the Jewban story.

THIRD GENERATION

Rachel B. is David's only daughter. She was born in Broward County, Florida. Her parents divorced when she was just one year old, so the way she was raised differed somewhat from the others in her generation.

Ashley is Perry's oldest daughter. She has done some research prior on the family tree and is inquisitive.

Scott is Ashley's husband. He is not Cuban but is Jewish and is interested in the family history. They just had a baby, Avery Skylar.

Stephanie is Perry's middle daughter. She worked for the organization Birthright for many years so is quite knowledgeable about Jewish history and Israel but less so about Cuban Jewish history.

Allan is Perry's youngest son. He is somewhat interested in Cuba today because he works in Major League Baseball and baseball is a passion in Cuba.

Paige is Lisette's oldest daughter. She expressed that she is not knowledgeable and knows much more about her dad's side than her mom's.

Dylan is Lisette's oldest son. Of this generation, he is the most knowledgeable about the family's history and the most interested in the Jewban experience.

Ethan is Lisette's youngest son, just finishing his first year at Vanderbilt University. He has more recently taken an interest in the family's history due to a course he took and a paper he had to write in which he interviewed a family member, Nathan (a cousin of Jack's), who had been separated from his mother during the Holocaust and raise in part by nuns in France.

DESCRIPTION OF THE CHAPTERS

In Part 1, I present a condensed history of the Jewban double diaspora. Chapter 1 focuses on Eastern European Jewish migration to Cuba. Although there was a small Cuban population on the island before the 1920s, it dramatically increased as Jews fled Eastern Europe due to antisemitism and lack of economic opportunity. My husband's grandparents all came at that time, and while all passed away well before I was part of the family, my research aimed to capture their stories the best I could through the recollections of their children and later generations as well as archival research and our own research in Cuba.

Chapter 2 features the stories and histories of Jewban exiles as a result of the Cuban revolution led by Fidel Castro in 1959. A double diaspora, as it has been described, this chapter highlights the reasons for the exodus, the receipt of Jewbans in the US., and their lives in yet another country. It provides, in brief, a historical review of the socio-political-economic factors that lead to the exodus. It also describes the emigres' reception in their new home. Although not exclusively about South Florida, the primary focus is on Jewbans located there. DiSipio noted that the pre-Revolutionary elite who made up the first wave of Cuban emigrants to Miami "brought with them higher levels of human capital than are customary in U.S. migration streams.

In Part 2, I share themes that emerged from interviews with three generations of Jewbans, all of which lived in South Florida for some time and most of whom still do.

Chapter 3 describes themes related to identity, family, and community that emerged from interviews with Jewbans. While prior research has found a strong Jewban identity, my research found a love of that title but more-so a Jewish, rather than Cuban, identity. This is connected to the diasporic history and socio-political situations both in Cuba and in the US.

Further, I emphasize what I have learned about community and how it was built and maintained amongst Jews in Cuba and Jewbans in South Florida. Unlike many immigrant groups in the US, Jewbans were able to develop and sustain community centers for their religious and cultural practices and thus helped keep a very close-knit community. Exiles in particular looked to recreate the closeness of their Jewish community in Cuba and then lived and taught this to their kids in South Florida and, to some extent, their grandchildren who remained in the area.

Additionally, the chapter emphasizes the importance of family. Immigration is very much about family, but even the opportunity to emigrate with family members, let alone their opportunities for success, is in such large part due to family ties. Family is typically a "hook" that allows immigrants to bring others to the US, and this is in particular true of the exiles from Cuba. Further, family ties help situate new immigrants into places where they may have a fresh start, which was a significant part of the Jewbans' success, at least of those I interviewed. And family money and connections help immigrants to find housing, jobs, and other resources, which is a significant part of the success of the Jewban diaspora.

In Chapter 4 I address risk-taking, work ethic and resilience. As a double diaspora that had to restart their lives in challenging conditions twice, the Jewbans are decidedly risk-takers, especially when it comes to starting businesses. As a demographic, the Jewbans have been tremendously successful in South Florida. As Disipio (2003) wrote, "Although the specifics of Cuban migrant adaptation are often assumed rather than analyzed, it is fair to say that they have achieved political and economic success more rapidly than other contemporary migrant populations" (p. 208). Interviewees repatedly stressed the emphasis of hard work, often at the expense of much leisure. Further, they emphasized the resilience of their people through each immigration transition. This, however, was more attributed to being Jewish than to being Jewban.

Chapter 5, "Idealized Cuba," discusses the memories of Cuba that have been passed along the generations of interviewees. All but one described pre-revolutionary Cuba in glowing terms. They tell of the island's beauty, its opportunities, and its lack of racism and other forms of discrimination. A read of history, however, suggests that this narrative may be through partially rose-colored glasses.

Part 2 addresses themes that were either minimally noted or not at all, yet would have been expected given social, historical and political history. In each chapter, I discuss why I believe these themes did not resonate with these interviewees.

Chapter 6 focuses on privilege. Much has been written about Cuban immigration privilege (See Eckstein, 2009; Eckstein, 2022). Immigration privileges were granted in the Cold War era and most remain today. These are privileges in status and benefits that were not afforded to any other immigrant group. The Cuban Relief Act, for instance, provided job training, cash assistance, employment opportunities, food, and various other forms of indirect aid to the state of Florida and to Miami Dade County (DiSipio, 2003). The interviewees were largely unaware of those privileges, even some of the exiles who were direct recipients.

Chapter 7 describes the political situation in Cuba post-exile through today. Again, interviewees professed to being largely unaware and generally disinterested despite the Cuban background. This is dissimilar from most immigrant groups, who have family and friends in their home country and who thus are incentivized to stay informed on current affairs.

In the Conclusion, I offer final comments from my position as a member of the family who is White, non-religious American with Irish and British roots. I also offer implications for peace educators and recommendations for future research.

REFERENCES

DiSipio, L. (2003). Cuban Miami: Seeking identity in a political borderland. *Latin American Research Review, 38*(2), 207–219.

Eckstein, S. (2009). *The immigrant divide: How Cubans changed the U.S. and their homeland.* Routledge.

Eckstein, S. (2022). *Cuban privilege: The making of immigrant inequality in America.* Cambridge University Press.

LaPorte, H., Schweifach, J., & Strug, D. (2003). Jewish life in Cuba today. *Journal of Jewish Communal Services, 84*(3/4), 313–324.

PART 1

HISTORY OF THE JEWBAN DIASPORA

CHAPTER 1

THE FIRST JEWS IN CUBA UNTIL REVOLUTIONARY CUBA

As an outsider, the idea that Eastern European immigrants fleeing persecution landed in Cuba was foreign to me. I was taught, as are most in the United States, that Americans were the big saviors of those seeking a better life. I had no idea Cuba had any role as a refuge for Jews. I guess I presumed that when people were leaving Eastern Europe due to pogroms and then the Holocaust, it was to come to the welcoming shores of the United States. It turns out that there is much about immigration policy in the United States in the 1920s through 1940s that I knew truly little about. As I expressed in the Introduction, I knew little about Cuba when I grew up in rural Michigan, so my images and ideas were all about a Caribbean island that was run by a brutal communist dictator. I did not have a sense of the history of Cuba, the population and why they were there, and how that related to US geopolitical, economic, and social issues. This was largely due to persecution during the 1900s, in particular the periods of the World Wars, although there was a small Jewish population on the island before those times. This chapter reviews what drove migration from Eastern Europe to Cuba, the experiences of Jews and their reception in Cuba, and significant policy decisions that shaped Jews' successes in their new home.

Shiksa Speaks: A White, Non-Jew's Understanding of the
Cuban Jewish Diaspora and Its Legacy, 3–25.
Copyright © 2025 *Laura Finley*
Published under exclusive licence by Emerald Publishing Limited
HB: 978-1-83708-494-4, PB: 978-1-83708-495-1, ePDF: 978-1-83708-496-8

David's maternal and paternal grandparents all left Eastern Europe—Belarus and Poland—for Cuba in the 1920s and 1930s. His paternal grandfather David Bekerman was born in Warsaw in 1902. Paternal grandmother Etel Marja Lederman Kusherman (birth date uncertain, but around 1905) was born in Kozienice, Poland. They arrived in Cuba some time in the 1920s. Image 1.1 is a photo of Eva and David. Etel took on the name Eva in Cuba. David's maternal grandparents Nachama Shapiro and Ycko (who became known as Isaac) Szczygiel arrived in Cuba in the 1930s. Image 1.2 is a photo of Nachama and Isaac. Nachama came as an eleven-year-old girl with her parents Leizer (also referred to as Lazaro) Shapiro and Basia, who became known as Berta (Dainowkski). Images 1.3 and 1.4 are of Nachama and Ycko's passports. Their motivation was to flee persecution, as is well documented and makes sense. However, they were also seeking new economic opportunities, as Cuba's economy was thriving. Like many, they intended to come to the United States eventually, but policy changes described in this chapter prevented them from doing so until after the Cuban Revolution. Lilia recalls how her parents and others in their generation described the hope that Cuba provided but also the challenges—new climate, culture, language, and more.

IMAGE 1.1.   David and Eva Bekerman

IMAGE 1.2.   Consuelo and Isaac Schigiel

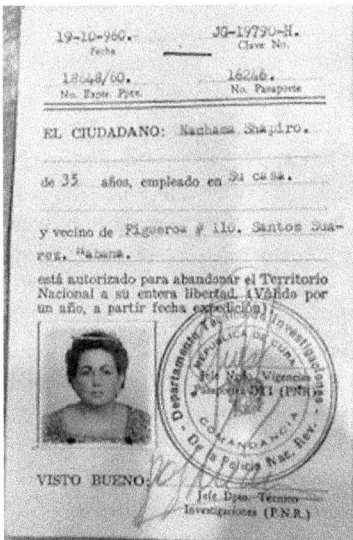

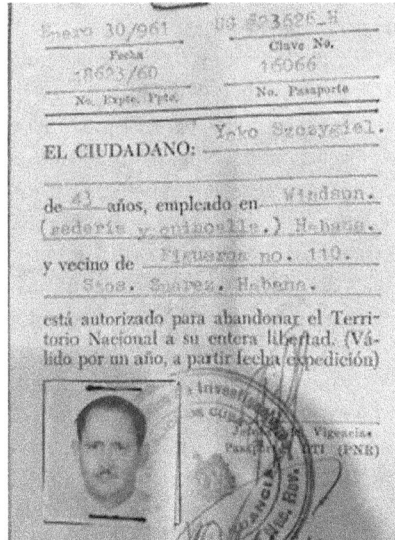

IMAGE 1.3.   Nachama Shapiro
Passport

IMAGE 1.4.   Ycko Szczygiel
Passport

BRIEF HISTORY OF JEWS IN CUBA PRE-1900

The earliest recorded Jew to visit Cuba came with Christopher Columbus. In March 1492, Ferdinand and Isabella of Spain issued the Alhambra decree, which required that all Jews in Spain convert to Christianity or be expelled by the end of July. There were approximately 300,000 Spanish Jews and the decree prompted an estimated 175,000 to leave Spain (Bannister, 2022). That same year, Luis de Torres, a Spanish Jew who had actually converted, was hired by Christopher Columbus to serve as an interpreter on his voyages. He is considered the first Jew to visit Cuba, which he did for four days doing their reconnaissance mission (Sarna, 1992). Two other Jewish converts were reportedly with de Torres, Juan de Cabrera and Rodrigo de Triano. Jews who converted, like these men, were called *marranos* or *conversos*. Many *conversos* settled in Cuba following de Torres, but little is known about them and their Jewish ancestry. Columbus described Cuba as "the loveliest land ever beheld by human eyes" (Levine, 1993, p. 8). The West Indies' Inquisition records contain lists of suspected Judaizers. One of those *marranos*, Hernando de Castro, built the first sugar mill near Santiago and is considered the pioneer of the sugar industry on the island (Shaland, 2017). In 1510, the Spanish conquered Cuba and in 1514 established the city of Santiago, which served as the capital from 1522 to 1563 before it was moved to the growing port city of Havana. Being Jewish was not allowed in Cuba at the time and to demonstrate one's Judaism could result in profound consequences, including death. In 1613 a man named Francisco Gomez de Leon was executed for "Judaizing" and his fortune was confiscated.

In the 16th and 17th century Jews fleeing from Portugal in Brazil landed in Cuba (Franklin, 2016). In 1762 the British briefly captured Havana but traded it to France in exchange for Florida just ten months later. For the most part, however, Cuba was under Spanish rule until nearly 1900. Known for its brutal Inquisition, Spain extended that to Cuba, its primary location in the Caribbean (Falcon, 2018). Puerto Rico and Cuba were the last strongholds for Spanish rule, as they were strategically essential to the imperialist country. Meanwhile Cuba was booming with the sugar trade. After the Inquisition was banned in Spain in 1834, Sephardic and some Ashkenazic Jews began to move to Cuba.

Slavery was a significant part of the development of the island's economy. This included the Indigenous Tainos as well as the Atlantic slave trade and later, slaves from China. More than 600,000 slaves were brought to Cuba in the 19th century (Hansing, 2018). Slavery in Cuba was an integral part in allowing the US to thrive. A greater percent of the 12.5 million enslaved Africans who were forced to come to the Americas from 1501 to 1867 were taken to Cuba than to North America—seven percent compared to four percent. Farber (2015) explained that, like in the United States, the darker a slave's skin, the worse he or she was treated. From 1847 to the 1880s, Chinese men were brought to the island to work on the sugar plantation amidst the ending of formal slavery. They were brutally exploited, perhaps worse than were the slaves before them. Slavery was abolished in Cuba in 1886, making it the second-to-last country in the Americas to abolish it (Behar, 1995. This was in large part due to Cuba's growing sugar industry and the country's belief that to outlaw slavery would put the economy in serious jeopardy (Bejarano, 1997). Farber (2015, p. 4) explained that

> slavery, in general, directly contributed to the expansion of capitalism. Furthermore, with this direct link to the future of capitalism, slavery also contributed to the onset of future issues and contingencies of racial, class and gender inequalities experienced throughout Cuba.

At this time, few Jews were on the island. Jewish immigrants were allowed to enter Cuba legally for the first time in 1881. The Catholic Church supported Spain and instilled hostility toward Jews in Cuba (Bejarano, 1997).

Most of the Jews in Cuba supported the effort for independence led by José Julián Martí y Pérez. Martí, as he is usually referred, was born to Spanish parents. His father was a Sargeant in the Spanish army, and his maternal grandfather was a decorated soldier for the Spanish military in Cuba. Martí, however, opposed Spain's colonial rule from an early age. As a teen, Martí was briefly a political prisoner because he wrote a letter to a peer discouraging him from joining the Spanish army. He was released and exiled to Spain, where he continued to write criticisms of Spanish colonialism in Cuba. Martí studied law in Spain, earning a law degree specializing in civil rights. After brief stints as a writer in Mexico and Guatemala, Martí returned to Cuba in 1878. After only a brief time he was accused of conspiring to overthrow Spanish rule and was again exiled to Spain. Martí then moved to New York City, where he continued to agitate for Cuban independence with other exiles. In 1895, Martí, Máximo Gómez, and Antonio Maceo Grajales launched an insurrection on the island, amassing a small group of guerillas to attack. Martí was killed but his efforts helped Cuba gain independence after the Spanish-American War in 1898 (Minster, 2019). In 1898 a cavalry led by Theodore Roosevelt stormed San Juan Hill, captured the city, thereby ending the Spanish American War and the Cuban War for Independence (Shaland, 2017). Franklin (2016), commented on the Jews support for Martí and independence.

> The one thing that the Jews subscribe to and speak openly about today is the teaching of José Martí. Fidel Castro is rarely mentioned, but Martí is highly visible in the common areas of all of the synagogues, either in the form of a bronze bust (as in the Patronado), on posters, in books, and in conversations (p. 16).

This observation is not consistent with what I found. None of the interviewees mentioned Martí nor had any visited any of the South Florida landmarks to him.

Martí and his comrades had support from American Jews, especially in South Florida, where many supported the Cuban Revolutionary Party (Bejarano, 1997). Although the island was free from Spanish rule, the Platt Amendment of 1901 gave the United States hegemonic power to intervene in Cuban affairs at any time in order to, "maintain a government adequate for the protection of life, liberty, and individual property[in Cuba]" (Piccone & Miller, 2016). It also granted the United States power to obtain property for a military naval base, which it holds to this day. It is the infamous Guantanamo Bay, whereas of this writing thirty detainees remain from the War on Terror after the September 11, 2001, terrorist attack. As a result of the Platt Amendment, Cuba was left controlling almost nothing on the island. All Cuban products were immediately exported to the United States. The US ensured as well that the Cuban government was revamped to align with U.S. interests (Piccone & Miller, 2016). The US wanted to purchase Cuba but was never able to do so, despite efforts by several presidential administrations (Ferrer, 2022). During these military occupations American Jews came to the island as soldiers, military suppliers, or merchants. Many were attracted by the opportunities for investment but when they arrived they intended to replicate their American environment in Cuba (Shaland, 2017). Cuba also became more open to immigration after the war. At the same time, economic and political instability in Europe drove many, including Jews, to leave. Steinberg (N.D.) maintains that Jews chose Cuba because it represented a chance for economic mobility and for religious acceptance. When the United States controlled Cuba, "race, class and gender issues continued to magnify, resulting in inequalities that are still apparent in the fabric of Cuban culture" (Farber, 2015, p. 14). While the US engaged in significant public works and infrastructure projects, including roads, bridges, power plants, schools, and more, many were unhappy that Cuba had "rid themselves of one colonial power but got another" (Powell, 2022, p. 7). Politically, the situation was somewhat chaotic in Cuba, as the island had fifteen permanent or interim presidents and two provisional governors sent by the US between 1902 and 1952, as well as many other changes (Powell, 2022).

JEWS IN CUBA, EARLY 1900s

Between 1902–1914 approximately 5,700 Jews, mostly Sephardim from Turkey and Syria, immigrated to Cuba. The island was attractive in part due to a surge in US investments that dramatically bolstered the sugar industry, offering many job opportunities, largely to young men. These Jews formed the first Jewish places of worship. Further, Cuba declared freedom of religion in its 1902 constitution. The Subsequent constitutions of 1928 and 1940 also enshrined freedom of religion and separation of church and state. These factors, coupled with its proximity to the US, made Cuba a welcome location for Jews fleeing persecution (Glaser, 2015). Ashkenazic American Jews began to arrive after the war for independence as well. In 1906, eleven US Jews formed the United Hebrew Congregation in Havana, which became the heart of the American Jewish community on the island. When Jews wanted to build a cemetery, they were denied, showing that the commitment to religious equality was not as firm as the government claimed. They then sought assistance from the United Hebrew Congregation which intervened because most of its members were American Jews (Bejarano, 1997). In 1910 the United Hebrew Congregation consecrated Beth Ha Haim, the first Jewish cemetery in Cuba. It was an arduous journey from Eastern Europe, and many who wanted to make the trip found it difficult to acquire the $100 needed for sea passage. Immigrants were required to have at least $10 when they landed. Kosher meals were tough to find on the ships so many observant Jews ate only bread and whatever they were able to bring on the ship (Franklin, 2016).

Many Ashkenazic Jews left Russia amidst the Bolshevik revolution. Lilia's grandfather Leizer Schapiro was one of them. He was a landowner, and his entire family was jailed and killed. He escaped through the Russia/Poland border. Lenin's government granted full access to vocational and educational opportunities but attempted to destroy Jewish culture. They promoted inter-religious and ethnic marriage, which contrasted with Jewish tradition. Some attempted to assimilate but others sought to migrate to more friendly environments. Eta (Eva's) family were well known in Koscieniz, as they operated a successful shoe factory (hence the name Lederman, which came from the word Leather which was used to make shoes). Eva was home-schooled by her mother, who taught her Yiddish and Hebrew. Her sister Mania was able to go to school for a few years, giving her more opportunities.

Early on, the Ashkenazic and Sephardic formed their own ethnic enclaves. In 1914 Sephardic Jews the Union Israelita Chevet Ahim, which was a synagogue but also provided assistance for the needy. The Sephardic had a slightly easier adjustment when it came to language, as many spoke Ladino, a Hebrew-Spanish blend. Further, their darker skin allowed them to blend in better in Cuban society. All faced difficulties adjusting and finding work, with most beginning as street peddlers. The tension was especially clear when Ashkenazic Jews were hesitant to allow Sephardic Jews to be buried in the Jewish cemetery because they considered the "Turks" to be uncivilized. In other ways the Sephardic suffered more. The United Hebrew Congregation, HIAS, and the JDC only provided help to Eastern European Jews (Bejarano, 1997). The norm for the first-generation children of Jewish immigrants to Cuba was to marry within the Jewish subcommunity. Intermarriages—those between an Ashkenazic and a Sephardic Jew—were frowned upon and marrying a non-Jew was unthinkable (Behar, 2007).

A portion of the Sephardic community identified with socialism. Some even participated in Communist activities. Several Sephardic and Ashkenazic Jews were among the founders of the Cuban Communist Party (Kaplan, 2001). Fabio Grobart, an Ashkenazi Jew, became one of the most well-known leaders (Bejarano, 1992).

JEWS IN CUBA, 1920s–30s

Ashkenazic immigration from Eastern Europe remained small through the World War I era. This changed between 1921 and 1924, when the US passed the Emergency Quota Act of 1921 and then the Immigration Act of 1924, which severely limited the number of Jews who could come to the US and made Cuba a preferred destination. Specifically, the Quota Act of 1921 limited each country to only three percent of foreign-born persons residing in the United States, using the 1910 census. At that time, the ratio of Europeans of northern and western origin versus southern and eastern was 5:4, which resulted in a favoring of immigrants from Northern and Western Europe, rather than those leaving Eastern Europe, which included many Ashkenazic Jews (Steinberg, N.D.).

> Influenced by concerns about the racial "fitness" of Southern and Eastern Europeans, this legislation was also inspired by fears that so-called aliens would import poverty and disease, as well as hostile foreign ideas like anarchism, Bolshevism and Catholicism. Migrants, consulates and border agents were immediately plunged into uncertainty as soon as Harding signed quota restrictions into law (Atkinson, 2017).

President Calvin Coolidge signed the National Origins Act in 1924. It imposed even more severe quotas on those coming from "undesirable" countries. One provision allowed individuals who lived in the western hemisphere for a year prior to immigrating to the United States to be exempt from the 1921. That increased to five years in 1922. In order to qualify for the exemption, many Eastern European Jews immigrated to Cuba. This became known as "akhsanie Kuba" (hotel Cuba), as the goal for most was never to stay on the island (Steinberg, ND, p. 5).

Simultaneous to these developments was a sharp decline in sugar prices. Some of the Jewish immigrants worked in the industry but found it difficult, as they were unaccustomed to the hot Cuban climate and the tough physical labor. A few found employment laying railways or at the ports, but most, as before, were peddlers (Bejarano, 1997).

Between 1921 and 1930, approximately 18,000 Jews fled from Eastern Europe to Cuba. Because there were so many single men from previous waves, Jewish mothers in Cuba began sending for women to make the trip. They were concerned that the men were starting to date non-Jewish Cuban women (Franklin, 2016). Eva Lederman traveled to Cuba in 1925 at the age of twenty. She was introduced to David Bekerman by an uncle who had gone into business with him and the two were soon married. Their daughter Sara, usually called Sarita, was born in 1929. Times in Cuba were difficult in the early 1930s due to the Great Depression as well as policies of the Machado government, so David traveled to Venezuela to try to get work and Eva took Sarita back to Poland then to Paris to visit Mania, Céline and Charlotte, Céline's sister. Something happened with French authorities and Eva had a tough time returning so David had to send telegrams and ship tickets to "keep her legal," Enrique recalls, although he does not know all the details. They moved back to Cuba in the mid-1930s and David brought over his mother and three sisters. Grandmother Pearl was widowed and had tried to support the girls in Poland, but it was difficult. All three girls eventually married and stayed in Cuba. Enrique describes his mother as truly kind and that she always honored and cherished the family. She also had a large extended family that was spread around the world, in Los Angeles, Colombia, Brazil, Belgium, Paris and other places. Eva always made a point of staying in touch with family via letters, sending photos, and phone calls. If anyone was in touch she would welcome them to her home. When his grandmother was older and frail, Enrique recalls his brother Jack carrying her up and down stairs so she could get to their store for a change of scenery.

On the other side of the family, sometime in the 1920s, the specific date unclear, Isaac's sister Ryfkah had come to Cuba with her husband. She was the first in the family to arrive on the island and it was she, somehow (details unclear) who helped Isaac flee Poland. They were the only two of nine siblings to survive the Holocaust and he forever felt indebted to her, much to his wife Consuelo's chagrin.

Sephardic Jews migrated during that time but had also emigrated steadily in the decades before, as noted above. The Ashkenazic Jews founded the Centro Hebreo in 1924. The Jews from Eastern Europe and Russia were familiar with socialism and largely disapproved, although there were a few supporters. Once in Cuba, those that accepted socialism separated from those who did not. Those that were more radical were involved with Centro Hebreo, which later became the Kultur Farain—Union Cultural Hebrew (Cultural Association—Hebrew Cultural Union) was created in 1925. It was largely a secular community group for leftist Jews who spoke Yiddish. Its membership was primarily working class and it engaged in antireligious propaganda (Bettinger-López, 2000). Kultur Farain was a gathering place for Jewish workers to share the Marxist ideology and to organize (Bejarano, 1997). Jewish communists also founded the Fonda Cooperative, a restaurant that also became a meeting place for Communist party members. Five Ashkenazi party members were killed between 1930 and 1933 as the Machado government cracked down on labor organizing. Several others, including Fabio Grobert, were expelled from the country. These actions eventually resulted in Kultur Farain shutting down in 1931, with it much of the Jewish support for communism (Bejarano, 1997).

Most Jews resided in the capital city of Havana, Cuba, but smaller communities could be found in other areas of the island, including Santiago de Cuba, Camaguey, Santa Clara, Matanzas, Cuantanamo, Cienfuegos, Caibarien, and Sancti Spiritus. Like the earlier Jews on the island, these new immigrants built social, cultural, and religious institutions. In 1922 the American Jewish Joint Distribution Committee (JDC, or el Joint, as Cubans call it), was established in Havana to aid Cuban Jews. The first Jewish day school was founded by a Sephardic Jew, Rabbi Guershon Maya in 1924. The first Ashkenazic synagogue, Adath Israel, was formed in 1925 and that same year the Centro Israelito merged several Jewish schools, eventually becoming the primary Jewish educational center on the island. The first Jewish High School, the Colegio Teodoro Herzl, was founded in 1926. In 1929 a second Ashkenazic synagogue, Knesseth Israel, was founded next door to Adath Israel.

Between 1925 and 1935, approximately 4,000 Eastern European Jews who spoke Yiddish, Polish and Russian, fled persecution and landed in Cuba. They found little antisemitism in their daily lives in Cuba and the opportunity for ample economic advancement. As is discussed in Chapter 7, however, there was indeed antisemitism on the island. They also received assistance from the JDC and another organization, the Hebrew Immigrant Aid Society (HIAS). But, as was discussed previously, the Jewish community in Cuba was fractured along ethnic lines. The Ashkenazi and Sephardic Jews found fault with one another and the American Jews on the island had little to do with either (Glaser, 2015). Additional aid to the Jewish immigrants came from National Council of Jewish Women in the U.S. Further, the Jewish Committee for Cuba, another American organization, served as a liaison for the new immigrants and provided assistance (Bejarano, 1997).

During the mid-1920s until 1933, the President of Cuba, Gerardo Machado, became increasingly tyrannical and in 1931 Jewish immigration to the island was halted. By this time, the Jews there had largely accepted that Cuba would be their home. Many had moved from peddling to establishing businesses, especially shoes and garments. Some of the Eastern European Jews had been trained as shoe-makers and tailors. They began to produce low quality goods at low prices, partly due to loans from American Jewish welfare associations. This allowed them to purchase the necessary equipment and machines. These businesses did well, as there was a lack of locally available mass-produced goods and imported goods were expensive. They were also helped by the 1927 Tariff Law which was intend-ed to increase local production, and Machado's explicit calls for Jewish entrepre-neurs to expand and establish new industries. These Jewish factories became the main source of employment for Eastern European immigrants (Bejarano, 1997).

After a wave of strikes and insurgencies, Machado was overthrown, and Ramón Grau San Martín became President. But, only for approximately one hun-dred days. Cuba was then led by Miguel Mariano Gomez and Federico Laredo Brú, but it was really military leader Fulgencio Batista pulling the strings. While there was much dissatisfaction with Batista, a rise in sugar prices that helped alleviate employment and renewed importation of American goods mitigated re-sentment and helped increase his popularity (Bejarano, 1997). In 1940, he became President of Cuba.

Many immigrants were devasted by San Martín's 1933 Law of Naturalization of Labor. It limited the salaried employment of immigrants in an attempt to build up Cuban businesses, requiring 50% of employees to be native-born. As a result, Jewish entrepreneurs innovated to work at home, to found cooperatives, and to open their own businesses. At least among the Ashkenazic. Prior to 1933, most shoes sold in Cuba were imported from America, as shoes that were produced on the island were made by hand and were considered expensive luxury items. Jews began opening up their own shops, producing cheap and functional shoes. Not long after, there were 150 shoe factories owned by Jews in Cuba. These facto-ries employed 6000 to 8000 workers (Steinberg, N.D.). The Sephardic, who were more often wage laborers, were hit harder by the law and were less able to adapt. Spanish merchants began a crusade of antisemitic publications that helped usher

IMAGE 1.5.   Israel Center of Cuba, 1954

in the law for their financial gain. Gestapo agents even paid some to spread Nazi propaganda to discourage Jewish immigration (Bejarano, 1992).

Jews could not become Cuban citizens in the 1920s. When they became able to attain citizenship in the 1930s, few could afford it. Many continued to receive assistance from organizations like HIAS and the JDC, as well as numerous other aid organizations (Behar, 2007; Franklin, 2016). Those I interviewed seemed unaware of the many help services that benefitted Jews, instead passing along a narrative that it was work ethic, risk taking and resilience that allowed the Jews to thrive. This is discussed in greater detail in Chapter 4. Most of the new Jewish immigrants recall being treated hospitably upon arrival, and in the 1930s a law passed allowing Jews to become Cuban citizens so many started to see it as more like home. Icko Szczygiel earned his Cuban citizenship in 1944, as documented in the Image 1.5. Bettinger-López (2000) explained, "Cuba's warm and friendly atmosphere allowed the Jews to develop tightly-knit Jewish communities while maintaining ties with Cubans from all walks of life and with the island nation itself" (p. xxxvii).However, records show, and these interviewees expressed, that these tight-knit Jewish communities were divided between American Jews, Ashkenazi immigrants, and Sephardic immigrants. Further, records do not show, nor did my interviews identify, significant interaction between the Jews in Cuba and other Cuba (Shaland, 2017).

The new immigrants to Cuba found that they did not make the wages they were used to in the industries available to them, hence many became self-employed as peddlers. In order to reduce costs and make more profits, many of these merchants bought raw materials abroad. Although many of the Eastern European Jews who went to Cuba in the 1920s–1940s began as peddlers on the streets, many became modestly successful merchants. They would take payment on installments which introduced a credit system (Behar, 2007). Thus, they transformed from peddlers to manufacturers, thereby moving from poor to middle class.

When David Bekerman arrived in Cuba in the 1920s as a young man, he struggled to make a living, working as an ice cream vendor and a shirt salesman before eventually opening a shoe factory. He met and married Eva Lederman in the 1920s and they married, with their daughter Sarita born in 1929. David was able to bring his mother and aunts from Poland to Cuba before the outbreak of World War II. He struggled with health issues, exacerbated by the hot, humid climate of Cuba. Enrique noted that David had several heart attacks and suffered from angina, such that by the time he was born David was barely able to work, nor could he walk far. Mother Eva became the primary breadwinner. David is described as both strict but warm, loving, and funny. Enrique recalls his father taking him often to the cinema and to buy Azucar Cande (sugar candy) and said he is glad they had great dentists in Cuba! He also recalls seeing films as a family, his father loving American movies with subtitles. His mother struggled to read them fast enough, so he recalls conversations in Yiddish as they discussed what was happening on the screen. Davis was also very honest and would get upset if someone took liberties with the truth. Well-read, David reviewed at least three newspapers each day. These included Diario de la Marina and Informacion in Spanish and Der Tog Morgen journal and Fovert in Yiddish.

Because there was such a huge presence of Jews from Poland during the 1920s and until the revolution, Cubans took to calling them Polacos, assuming all Jews were from the same country. Yiddish was called *el idioma polaco*, the Polish language. The terms remain in use on the island today, despite there being few Jews remaining. Cuba's elites were happy with the influx, as they sought to "whiten" the island amidst uprisings amongst Blacks in neighboring countries. Jewish immigrants "brought intense ideological commitments and were divided between those who favored Zionism and those who thought the Jewish future depended on international ideals of socialism, communism, and atheism" (Behar, 2007, p. 6). Cuban Jews in the 1930s were divided between Zionism and Communism, or at least leftism. Union Sionista, or Zionist Union, which consisted of Zionists who supported a Jewish state in Israel. Gezelshaft far Kunst und Kultur (Society for Art and Culture) was dominated by Communists but included other left-leaning members. The dominant organization, however, Centro Israelita, remained neutral. More Sephardic Jews participated in the former, initially, and their efforts resulted in the Teodoro Hertzl School. As more Ashkenazic joined the Zionist movement the Sephardic splintered off, and Ashkenazi Jews began to lead the movement (Bejarano, 1997).

Ester recalls their family's narrative of leaving Eastern Europe.

In Abuela Berta's family mythology, stories of shtetl hardship paved the way for the family's creation myth, her decision to undertake the arduous journey out of Eastern Europe in 1936 and book passage to Cuba. The family's voyage, like any heroic quest, required that we outwit a cruel, arbitrary fate whose small coincidences and near misses obscured the enormous consequences. If we could catch the appointed train, we could begin a passage ending in a land of palm trees and plenty. If we missed the many necessary connections, we would leave the shtetl on a different train, and remain forever in Poland, strewn as smoke and ashes in Hitler's crematoria. (pp. 230–231)

Berta also told how her own daughter Consuelo increased the danger of the trip, as she was purportedly in need of constant maternal vigilance. Ester wondered why that was, and how Consuelo came to be excluded or at least minimized from the family's inner circle. In reality, as Ester explained, it was her passionate intensity and vivid curiosity that made her an ill fit for the conservative family. Consuelo saw the trip as an exciting adventure compared to their boring shtetl lives. She is said to have evaded her parents along the way and took her brothers wandering London, only to make it back to their hotel because they were lucky enough to find someone who spoke Yiddish to give them directions. The long trip on the ship in crowded third class was tough for the family. Ester's father Jaime was just six and his brother Neiach (later Noel) was nine. They followed their sociable sister around, and she charmed the crew into giving them better accommodation and many benefits. They had regular access to first-class meals.

JEWS IN CUBA, 1930s AND 40s

The final large wave of Jewish immigration to Cuba occurred in the late 1930s, as Jews fled persecution from the Nazis. Between 1938 and 1939, approximately five hundred German-speaking Jews came to Cuba each month. Several thousand more came during the next several years. Most of these German Jews never became integrated into the Jewish community and left for the United States when World War II ended (Levinson, 2006). As more Jews fled Europe after Kristallnacht pogroms on November 9 and 10 of 1939, they found entry to the US and to Cuba to be strictly limited. At this time, in contrast to the utopia described by the exiles I interviewed.

Skin color determined to a large degree one's social as well as economic status: blacks and mulattos stood at the bottom of the ladder, in both rural and urban Cuba. This prejudice may have been one unstated reason why Jewish immigrants were able to succeed in as few years as they did. (Levine, 2010, p. 63)

A significant marker in Cuban Jewish life was the St. Louis incident. By the end of 1938, Cuba, like many other countries, faced a dilemma; it had been accepting streams of Jews fleeing Nazi Europe and there was a growing tide of opposition. This was in part due to fascist and Nazi propaganda as well as concern that Jews were taking jobs from Cubans. Radio pronouncements in Cuba referred to Jews as "human garbage" (Levine, 2010, p. 79). The US also advised against sending more refugees to Cuba. Under Reich propaganda minister Joseph Goebbels, fourteen German agents were sent to Cuba to stir up public opinion against Jewish refugees. The larger plan was to permit a group of Jews to leave Germany, then

> trumpet their undesirability, and then pressure countries not to take them in. The principal vessel selected to carry out this scenario was the Hamburg-Amerika line's handsome, 575-foot luxury liner *SS St. Louis*, one of the fastest and largest motorships in Europe. (Levine, 2010, p. 103)

These efforts proved effective, as President Laredo Bru, who had previously promoted acceptance of most any refugees, asked Congress to prohibit immigration of "Hebrews" who had been inundating the Island. Congress then restricted all foreigners except US citizens and required of them a bond of $500 and authorization by the Cuban secretaries of state and labor. All permits and visas issued before the May 5, 1939, decree were retroactively invalidated. The St. Louis carried 937 refugees. It was to arrive along with two smaller boats the first week of June 1939. Passengers were required to purchase a round-trip ticket even though they did not intend to return. This was simply a money grab. In Cuba, Colonel Manuel Benitez, head of immigration, made a fortune on issuing landing permits to the refugees. It is not entirely clear whether he knew that these would later be considered invalid. What none of the refugees knew, nor did Captain Schroeder, was that the Cuban government's decree had retroactively invalidated their landing permits just eight days before they set sail. The voyage was a deliberate Nazi attempt to assess other countries' willingness to accept refugees, with the hope that no one would accept them (Levine, 2010).

In Cuba, the Cuban Nazi party issued allegations that the refugees were communist. These were reprinted in virtually every Cuban newspaper. Daily reports about the St. Louis whipped up anti-refugee sentiment and prompted the island's largest antisemitic protest. A rally against their arrival drew some 40,000 attendees, with tens of thousands more listening via radio. Cuban-Jewish groups organized to counter these attacks. In fact, nineteen diverse groups came together, the first time ever all segments of Jewish society had met under one roof. They established the Fareiningten Komitet Zum Bakemfn dem Antisemitism in Kuba (the United Committee to Combat Anti-Semitism in Cuba) and the Comite Central de las Sociedades Hebreas de Cuba (Central Bureau of Jewish Organizations in Cuba), both of which focused, to no avail, on acquiring permission for the refugees on the St. Louis to enter Cuba. In-fighting likely impacted their efforts (Levine, 2010).

On May 24, 1939, Cuban newspapers issued a dispatch from the German embassy announcing that the St. Louis had set sail and was carrying 1,000 refugees. When President Bru heard about their forthcoming arrival despite the decree, he set into motion a series of steps designed to turn the ship away. The ship dropped anchor on May 27, but it was denied permission to dock in the typical area and none of the passengers were permitted to disembark. For six days the St, Louis and its passengers broiled in the harbor in 102-degree heat, Family members tried to reach their relatives on the ship, taking small boats out to at least shout encouragement to them. The only people permitted to board the ship were police officers (as Captain Schroeder had requested twenty-five port police, fearing unrest), certain medical officers, representatives of the ship's line, Jewish Relief Committee head Milton D. Goldsmith, and Rabbi Meir Lasker of the American Jewish congregation. Many passengers suffered illness, depression, and became hysterical. Cuban public opinion overwhelmingly supported the government's refusal to let the ship land and its passengers disembark. Only a few were actually permitted to leave the ship, which included twenty-two with regularly issued visas (Levine, 2010).

On June 2, President Bru demanded that the St. Louis leave Cuban waters or be towed if it did not. On June 6, Captain Schroeder turned the ship around to turbulent waters. It sailed as close to South Florida as possible and anchored briefly off Miami Beach but was not granted permission to dock. Diplomatic relations ensued to see who would take the refugees, with Belgium finally agreeing to accept some and the Dutch and British some as well. The French government agreed to take the remainder. The St, Louis landed in Antwerp on June 17 and the passengers were taken by train to security. When Belgium fell to the Nazis, some these refugees remained hidden and some escaped or survived the Holocaust. Others perished in the camps. Similar fates awaited the others. The refusal of the US and Canadian governments to help the Jewish refugees was a propaganda win for the Nazis. In all, 254 of the 907 passengers on the St. Louis perished as part of the final solution. Subsequent to this, for a time, only the very affluent were able to purchase illegal documents to leave Eastern Europe and end up in Latin America (Levine, 2010).

Marion Kreith, who fled the Holocaust to Cuba and thought it to be a temporary stop, expressed in the documentary *Cuba's Forgotten Jewels*, "It was a very, very fortunate way of escaping being exterminated." She worked in the diamond industry, which was a thriving industry on the island. She had a tough time leaving Europe. She was born in Germany and tried to escape in 1938. In 1941 they went illegally from occupied Belgium to unoccupied southern France and then to Spain and Portugal before getting on a boat to Cuba. I would have loved to hear the stories of the travels of Eva, David, Isaac, and Consuelo but was not able to get much information about their arduous trips from Poland to Cuba. Kreith, however, explained that she was totally unaware of how dangerous it was. She recalls an intellectual from Berlin walking around the ship asking if anyone has read Mein Kampf. Everyone was horrified, but he was disturbed that no one was really aware or concerned with what was happening. Once in Cuba her family became part of a Zionist organization and she recalls that she, like David's family, was generally unaware of a lot of what was happening because they were in their own bubble. She admits that their interaction with the Cuban people was quite limited, and pretty much the result of having Cuban workers. No one I interviewed expressed this explicitly, but from what I could tell, the same was true. No one remains connected to anyone in Cuba nor has spoken of Cuban friends who were not Jewish. Kreith said she was never in the home of a Cuban family, nor do I believe anyone in my husband's family to have done so. There was little intermingling of social life between the Jewish immigrants and the Cubans. Her family was only there in the 1940s but she observed that the one issue that needed to be addressed was the disparity between rich and poor. She called it "a complete dichotomy between the haves and the have nots." She recalls her lasting emotions of gratitude for being accepted in Cuba. Lilia and Jack and their family seemed to express the same sentiments about Cuba, so it surprised me how little any of them cared or care for Cuba today, as is discussed in Chapter 8.

Nathan Spiewak is David's paternal grandmother's nephew, her sister Mania's son. His last name means singer, although he said he has no singing voice. He was born in Paris in 1933. His parents were born in Poland and tried to find a safe space in Europe to raise their only child. It seems the family had money, as he described a nice apartment, attending summer camps, and having a full-time maid, but this did not save them from persecution. Nathan described himself as a happy child, spoiled as he was the only one, and without a worry. His dad had a small successful business, and his mother was a high fashion designer for wealthy women. The happiness was disrupted as the Nazis began forbidding Jews from doing much and he recalls being made fun of at school and spit at because they had to wear the yellow star. French police and Gestapo would routinely come to the school to ensure that all the Jewish students were wearing their yellow stars. When his father had to go to work sewing rabbit fur into jackets to be worn by Nazis, they found a small way of being subversive—they ensured that after a brief time the linings would come apart at the seams. Nathan recalls mass round ups of Jews before they were moved to concentration camps. On July 16, 1942, French police came to their apartment and arrested him and his mother. His father was at work. They were pushed onto a crowded bus then taken to a processing space where they waited for hours and had to have all of their jewelry confiscated. Everyone there was crying and yelling, and his mother and he found a corner to sleep in for the next few days. The toilet overflowed and he said the stink was unbearable. She had packed some food, so they shared with others; otherwise, they had to wait in line for bread, cheese and occasionally soup. They were released after five days due to the orchestrations of his father, who gave a lot of money to some people at his company who had influence. The Nazis took more than 13,000 people,

Spiewak recalls. One month later the French police came again and gave them half an hour to pack one suitcase before they were taken to be with "people of their own kind." As they walked through a crowded street his parents pushed him into the crowd and told him to run. He walked miles and miles and family friends let him stay there for seven days, hiding in a small closet under the stairs. They contacted a cousin in a different part of France that was not occupied by the Nazis.

His cousin Céline, Eva's niece, and her brother Jack came and got him at the end of 1942, told him to remove the yellow star, and gave him a new name, Jean. Two weeks after this the family that housed him were sent to a concentration camp, never to return. It took the three of them seven days to reach Nice, in the South of France. Céline was dating an Italian officer who knew they were Jews but did not turn them in. They later married and sent him to Catholic school for three months. He ran away three times because he was always hungry, as the school did not have enough food for all the Jewish refugees that were also hiding. In 1943 the Americans invaded Sicily. Approximately two thousand Jews and non-Jews crossed to Italy. Another cousin, Claire, took him with her on the travel. They had little clothes and it got very cold. After two days of walking, they spotted an empty cabin that was used by hunters, so they were able to get some rest. It took several days of walking to cross the mountains. They were welcomed to a small Italian village, where the villages fed them well. Claire and her boyfriend Bernard went to buy some baked goods at a bakery and the baker took him next door to the shoemaker to get a pair of wooden shoes to replace his sandals. The baker asked if he could stay with them and help him in the bakery. Spiewak was treated well there, as they fed, dressed, and cared for him. One day they went for a picnic and saw German tanks and soldiers surrounding the village. They were rounding up and arresting people. Claire said they should return to Nice. She sent him to their apartment to get as many clothes as they could so they could leave. He was stopped by two Germans along the way. All the people that were captured in that village were sent to concentration camps. Most died. He and Claire got lost on their way and were very hungry. On the third day they were surrounded by masked men with guns. It turns out they were with an underground group that tried to help Jews escape. When they finally arrived back in Nice, he was picked up by an uncle. The first thing he did was put the yellow star back on Nathan. His uncle contacted an organization that helped place Jewish kids with non-Jewish families and he was placed with a couple living in a small village. He spent nine months there on their farm, where they introduced him as their nephew who had lost his parents in the war. They enrolled him a Catholic school run by nuns. He had to go to church every Sunday. Every now and then Germans would come to confiscate animals from the farms so they could feed the troops. His parents had been sent to Auschwitz separately and both spent time in other camps, including Dachau. They did not see each other for three years. At Auschwitz, his father had to take dead people from the gas chamber to the crematorium. At the end of 1944 Jews in the Warsaw Ghetto fought against the Nazis. His father was sent there with some other Jews from the camps to clean up the destroyed ghetto after some thirty days of uprising. Some prisoners escaped but most were captured. A week before the end of the war his father and some others were sent back to Auschwitz, where they were to be killed. They escaped along the way, and they made their way to a small village. The soldiers pursued them, and his father and two others ran back to the train. All three were shot, his father in the shoulder. He laid down and pretended he was dead, as the soldiers were shooting the wounded to make sure they were dead. When he made it back to the train it was now under the control of American soldiers. He was taken to a doctor but originally refused care because the doctor was German, but he eventually got help from a Jewish doctor. At the end of the way he waited with his uncle in Paris, hoping to hear something about his parents. They read the newspaper every day for the listing of survivors who had been released from the camps. One day his aunt woke him up he saw a strange man sitting at the table, wearing prisoner clothing. It was his father. His mother was part of an exchange of French women for German soldiers. Although she was Polish, she pulled it off and after a few months in Switzerland she came home to Paris. They soon joined his Eva and her family in Cuba. They then moved to the United States in 1951. Since 1957 Nathan has been receiving compensation from the German government. In all, he lost forty members of his family to the Holocaust. His father passed away in Cuba in 1948 from the suffering he endured in the camp. His mother passed away in 1996.

It would seem that escaping the Holocaust would bring Jews together, wherever they were. But this did not seem to be the case in Cuba. Glaser (2015) asserted that rather than unifying Jews in countries like the US and Cuba, the Holocaust weakened bonds, as too many people vied for too few resources and Jews already in these places feared that the destitute refugees would incite antisemitism that would affect them as well. Rather than contributing to assist the refugees, local Jews instead erected obstacles. Tensions increased as the newcomers had to stay longer and longer due to the changes in immigration laws in the US. Conflicts emerged between Ashkenazi and Sephardic Jews, between Zionists and non-Zionists, and between liberal and orthodox Jews. The refugees struggled with the new language, climate, separation from family and loss of their livelihood (Glaser, 2015). Lilia said her mother told her about wearing thick coats that were way too hot for the humic Cuban climate, but it was what they had from Poland.

1940 saw a large group of Jewish diamond workers from Antwerp and Amsterdam seeking refuge in Vedado, just outside of Havana. They built their own school, synagogue, mikvah (ritual bath) and established a soon thriving diamond business. This group of Jews thrived because they

> were able literally to bring the diamond industry with them because it required little equipment beyond cutting and polishing machines, which could be manufactured anywhere; prototype machines were imported from Brazil and then copied. The labor was manual and precise. (Levine, 2010, p. 162)

The burgeoning industry employed hundreds of workers, virtually all of whom were Jewish refugees although it did employ some native Cubans. Someone in the Bekerman extended family engaged in this industry but I was unable to track down the details.

As Cuban Jews became more prosperous in the mid to late 1940s, many moved to the suburbs like Vedado. By 1948, most Jews in Cuba were considered among the middle class (Steinberg, N.D.). By 1949, there were an estimated 12,000 Jews in Cuba, with 8, 500 residing in Havana (Levinson, 2006), and in the 1950s approximately 30,000 Jews resided in Cuba (Dolsten, 2016). The growing Ashkenazic population built the Patronato de la Case de la Communidad Hebrea, which served as a synagogue and community center. The Patronato, built in 1953, was not uniformly supported by Cuba's Jews. Jewish leaders in old Havana opposed it. Newly affluent Jews in the suburbs were able to raise between $750,000 and $1 million for the construction of the center (Kaplan, 2001). Many Jews who went to the Patronato did so less for religious observance and more for cultural or social activities (Laporte et al., 2009). Levine (2010) reported that Cuban Jews used their White skin to their advantage and were largely middle class if not more affluent. "Visitors compared parties given by members of high society . . . to those of Aristotle Onassis . . . Mink, chinchilla, sable, and ermine furs were popular... in 1946" (Levine, 2010, p. 205).

David's great grandmother Berta's sister Anita married into the Garmizo family, and they went into the sugarcane business with Consuelo's brothers Jaime and Noel Shapiro. It was successful in Cuba and when they left the island, they established the business in South Florida which is still flourishing today, run by Jaime and Noel's grandkids.

In the later 1940s, Enrique said that he aunt Mania and her cousin Charlotte has been liberated from concentration camps. Cousin Celine had hidden through the war and stayed in Paris, where she started a successful fashion house. Charlotte returned to Paris as well, while Mania, her husband, and his cousin Nate (Spiewak, discussed above) reunited after the war and came to Cuba to live with the Bekermans for a couple of years. Mania's husband suffered from the experience in the camps and passed away. Mania and Nate then moved to Los Angeles in the early 1950s. She remarried and Louis later became Enrique's legal guardian when the family left Cuba and he ended up in Los Angeles. In Cuba, Mania helped Eva to grow their dress factory. She had been a dressmaker in Paris. Jack was very involved in the business in the 1950s, as he made dress deliveries, collected monies, and did other tasks. Modas Ethel was extraordinarily successful and became a huge part of Eva's identity. By the mid-1950s the family was able to move to a nice area of Havana called Miramar.

Consuelo Shapiro and Icko (now Isaac) Szczygiel (now Schiegel) married in Matanzas, Cuba in 1942, when she was just seventeen. One year later Lilia was born. A family "secret" is that Consuelo had been married before, in an arranged marriage when she was fifteen and still in Poland. He was much older, and the official paperwork says they divorced although Lilia says the marriage was annulled. She had no idea about this until she herself was married and she found a photograph of her mother with the other person cut out—that was her husband. Consuelo's family did not like Isaac as he drank a lot and did not come from much money, according to several family members.

ROAD TO REVOLUTION

For many in Cuba, the Batista days were good. Some demographics were doing well financially, and the island was a vibrant party paradise. Yet he was always a controversial figure, first as a de factor leader, then as elected president in 1940, then later after resigning and retiring in Florida only to return to the island and take over in a coup in 1952. While reports are that Batista's earlier days saw him engaged in progressive politics, his return to Cuba was characterized by his efforts to gain the acceptance of the upper classes. The elite had denied Batista access to their upper echelon events and activities, and he sought to remedy that, focusing on acquiring wealth. To that end, Batista associated with some dubious characters, including heads of organized crime like Meyer Lansky, a Jew (born Maier Suchowljansky in 1902 in what is now Belarus). While Cuba had an official national lottery during Spanish colonial times, casinos began to develop in Cuba in the 1920s as tourism grew (Jacobin). In the 1940s and 1950s Batista opened the island up to gambling and announced that the government would match, dollar for dollar, investments in Cuban hotels over $1 million. One author described Cuba under Batista "as hopelessly corrupt, a Mafia playground, a bordello for Americans and other foreigner" (Farber, 2015). While his administration sponsored some important infrastructure developments—an underwater tunnel, the Veradero highway, train lines, and more—it was largely funded by dirty mob money. The Batista regime used Cuban state development banks and even union retirement funds to pay for these developments. Even still, it was the sugar industry that generated most of the island's profits, as widespread commercial travel was not really available to most (Farber, 2015), Those who were doing well were, it seems, quite willing to overlook the graft. Or never questioned how and why things were the way they were. As I understand, the general social status of this family made them less inclined to be worried about the corruption and problems with Batista than were others less similarly situated. In general, it was mostly Americans and other tourists who gambled in them. Although Jews, Blacks, and the lower classes were not allowed in certain clubs, according to Enrique, it is clear that this family did not suffer tremendous discrimination in Cuba. Lilia remembers going to the famous, dazzling Tropicana nightclub for her birthday when she was fifteen, she thinks. The Tropicana, which debuted in 1956, was the epitome of glitz and glamour. It was affluence at its best and known as the "Cabaret in the sky"—a sensual song, dance, and dinner show that was and remains way out of the price range of most people. She did not seem to know that the Tropicana was ground zero for the mafia.

Another issue that was not brought up by my interviewees but that was common in Cuba during this time period and before was sex work. By the time of the revolution, an estimated 11,500 women earned their living as sex workers in some 270 brothels. This was one of few occupations available to poor women, with domestic work being the primary option. This too was pretty much accepted and not a significant part of the critique of Batista and his regime. The people interviewed for this book, however, did not describe that any female members were engaged in either. Rather, their families employed maids (Farber, 2015).

While some American liberals and radicals saw gambling and prostitution as evidence of what was wrong with 1950s Cuba, the corruption and excesses were not the primary reason for dissatisfaction with Batista and his regime. Rather, there was considerable concern that Batista's henchmen had engaged in torture and murder, the high rates of unemployment and poverty in rural areas, and the one-crop economy were of bigger concern (Farber, 2015). Fidel Castro promised to rectify these things. For example, after the failed attack he led on the Moncada military barracks in Eastern Cuba, Castro was tried and delivered a speech titled "History Will Absolve Me." In it he vowed to make agrarian reforms to allow small land allotments to landless peasants but also to compensate landlords. He also called for workers in large industrial, mercantile, and mining industries—including sugar—to receive 30 percent of profits. Further, Castro vowed to nationalize the electric and telephone companies and to confiscate the wealth of those like Batista, who had misappropriated public funds. Thus, albeit critical of the runaway grift on the island, Castro and his revolutionaries saw it as secondary to, and emblematic of, deeper structural and systemic (Farber, 2015).

But amongst others who were suffering or even targeted by the Batista regime, his growing unpopularity in the early 1950s was neither surprising nor unwelcome. Batista was, as Piccone and Miller (2016) explained, an "unofficial" spy for the United States, using his influence to serve US interests. Some Cubans, especially those in rural areas, lived in abysmal poverty. They were malnourished, constantly hungry, and often in debt that seemed insurmountable. One analyst commented,

> One might best summarize the complex situation by saying that urban Cuba had come to resemble a Southern European country (with a living standard as high or surpassing that of France, Spain, Portugal and Greece) while rural Cuba replicated the conditions of other plantation societies in Latin America and the Caribbean. (American Experience, n.d.)

As Parker (2015) explained,

> By the early 1950s, throughout the island, with the exception of the elite, most Cubans lived in impoverished, squalor-like conditions. The United States on the other hand, continued to prosper at the expense of Cuba. New sugar mills were constructed to assist with the increased capitalistic, exploitative role and also contributed to the new railways throughout Cuba to transport goods to other cities outside of

Havana. Several American companies and banks were also established in Cuba, thereby creating an American fortress away from the mainland. (p. 35)

Most Jews did not participate in the Revolution. One theory as to why is that they were still largely acclimatizing to the island and were not yet confident enough about their identity within the country to be involved in any kind of radical social change movement (Kaplan, 2001). As Shaland (2017) expressed, "Most Cuban Jews stayed away from the dangerous politics in their home-island. They were well off and content, and they wanted their tiny secure "islands" to last for eternity." Further, as is discussed in subsequent chapters, Castro himself was not antisemitic and in fact, took specific measures to accommodate Jews. Many records indicate that he was of Jewish origin, from his grandmothers of Spanish Galicia and the Canary Islands (Shaland, 2017). Enrique remembers that his father David, a scholar of history, saw the signs of Castro's intent early on, much to his dismay. Enrique remembers being infatuated "with the bearded demigods that came down from the mountains with Pancho Villa style bullet 'garlands" around their necks." He said most of the island felt the same way. Marcos recalls people flooding the streets with excitement over the prospect of change after seven years of a corrupt dictator and harsh military repression. The excitement quickly turned to concern, especially among middle and upper classes who did not want their businesses expropriated. People feared they were being spied on and targeted as enemies of the revolution and heard rumors that the Castro regime might send their children to labor camps or to the Soviet Union. These things and much more made the extended family ready themselves to flee their new home.

CONCLUSION

This chapter provided a brief review of Cuban history, focusing on the growth of the Jewish population on the island. It discussed the trajectory of David's family's immigration to Cuba, their reception there, and then the developments that led to Castro's revolution, which uprooted the family once more.

REFERENCES

American Experience. (n.d.). *Pre-Castro Cuba. PBS.* https://www.pbs.org/wgbh/american-experience/features/comandante-pre-castro-cuba/

Atkinson, D. (2017, February 3). What history can tell us about the fallout from restricting immigration. *Time.* https://time.com/4659392/history-fallout-restricting-immigration/

Bannister, M. (2022). A 1492 letter regarding Jewish property in Spain. *Museum of Jewish Heritage.* https://mjhnyc.org/blog/1492-letter-regarding-jewish-property-in-spain/#:~:text=In%201492%2C%20King%20Ferdinand%20and,their%20thousand%2Dyear%20homeland%20behind.

Behar, R. (1995). Introduction. In R. Behar (Ed.) *Bridges to Cuba/Puentes a Cuba* (pp. 1–20). University of Michigan Press.

Behar, R. (2007). *An island called home: Returning to Jewish Cuba.* Rutgers University Press.

Bejarano, M. (1992). *The Jewish community of Cuba 1898–1939: Communal consolidation and trends of integration under the impact of changes in world Jewry and Cuban society.* Thesis submitted to Hebrew University, Jerusalem. https://www.latinamericanstudies.org/cuba/Jewish_Community_Cuba-1898-1939.pdf

Bejarano, M. (1997). *From Havana to Miami: The Cuban Jewish community.* AMILAT. https://amilat.online/wp-content/uploads/2020/01/Margalit-Bejarano-3-113.pdf

Bettinger-López, C. (2000). *Cuban-Jewish journeys: Searching for identity, home, and history in Miami.* University of Tennessee Press.

Dolsten, J. (2016). 7 moments that define Castros ties with Jews. *Times of Israel.* https://www.timesofisrael.com/7-moments-that-defined-castros-relationship-with-jews/

Falcon, L. (2018, October 4). *Manufacturing sin: The Inquisition in Cuba between 1604 and 1614.* Florida International University Cuban Research Institute Events.

Farber, S. (2015, September). Cuba before the revolution. *Jacobin.* https://jacobin.com/2015/09/cuban-revolution-fidel-castro-casinos-batista4

Ferrer, A. (2022). *Cuba: An American history.* Scribner.

Franklin, D. (2016). *The Jewish lived experience in Cuba.* Dissertation for The University of Alabama. https://ir-api.ua.edu/api/core/bitstreams/d86bf9a7-5c95-4424-9577-6032807c70b0/content

Glaser, Z. (2015). *Refugees and relief: The American Jewish Joint Distribution Committee and European Jews in Cuba and Shanghai, 1938–1943.* Dissertation for the City University of New York. https://academicworks.cuny.edu/cgi/viewcontent.cgi?article=1560&context=gc_etds

Hansing, K. (2018). Race and rising inequality in Cuba. *Current History, 117*(796), 69–72.

Kaplan. D. (2001). *The Jews of Cuba since the Castro revolution.* American Jewish Year Book. https://www.bjpa.org/content/upload/bjpa/101c/101cuba.pdf

Laporte, H., Sweifach, J., & Strug, D. (2009). Jewish life in Cuba today. *Journal of Jewish Communal Service, 84*(3/4), 313–324.

Levine, R. (2010). *Tropical diaspora: The Jewish experience in Cuba.* Markus Wiener Publishers.

Levinson, J. (2006). *Jewish community of Cuba: The golden years: 1906–1958.* Westview.

Minster, C. (2019, May 15). *Biography of Jose Marti, Cuba poet, patriot, revolutionary.* Thoughtco. https://www.thoughtco.com/biography-of-jose-marti-2136381

Piccone, T., & Miller, A. (2016, December 19). *Cuba, the U.S., and the concept of sovereignty: Toward a common vocabulary?* Brookings Institute. https://www.brookings.edu/articles/cuba-the-u-s-and-the-concept-of-sovereignty-toward-a-common-vocabulary/

Powell, D. (2022). *Ninety miles and a lifetime away: Memories of early Cuban exiles.* University of Florida Press.

Sarna, J. (1992). *Columbus & the Jews.* Brandeis University https://www.brandeis.edu/hornstein/sarna/americanjewishcultureandscholarship/Archive6/Columbusandthe-Jews.pdf

Shaland, I. (2017, December 20). The island within an island: Cuba's Jewish history. *Moment Magazine.* https://momentmag.com/island-within-island-cubas-jewish-history/

CHAPTER 2

JEWBAN EXILES FROM THE REVOLUTION

This chapter begins with the revolution that overthrew Fulgencio Batista and resulted in Fidel Castro taking power in Cuba. It provides a brief review of the revolution, its immediate effects, and its reception by Cubans. It then focuses specifically on how Cuba's Jews responded, which for most was to flee the country. In the chapter I share the "leaving" stories of some of the exiles I interviewed. Additionally, I tell of their early experiences in their new home country, the United States.

Prior to 1959, Cuba was largely a country that received people from other countries, not a sender of them. This is with a few exceptions. By the 1820s sizeable groups of Cubans had migrated to New York City, Philadelphia, and New Orleans, most of whom were professionals or merchants. More emigrated to the US during the Ten Years War (1868–1878), the Little War (1879–1880), and the Cuban War of Independence (1895–1898). Approximately 55,700 Cubans migrated to the US between 1868 and 1898, many skilled workers but others seeking political refuge amidst the wars with Spain. Skilled cigar workers landed in Key West and Tampa, Florida, New York City, and New Orleans. New York was the hub for much of the Cuban immigrants, with the air service between New York City and

Shiksa Speaks: A White, Non-Jew's Understanding of the
Cuban Jewish Diaspora and Its Legacy, 27–47.
Copyright © 2025 *Laura Finley*
Published under exclusive licence by Emerald Publishing Limited
HB: 978-1-83708-494-4, PB: 978-1-83708-495-1, ePDF: 978-1-83708-496-8

Havana one of the busiest routes in North America (Perez, 2018). Cuba and the US had, as was described in Chapter 1, a relationship that was financial and political. Not everyone was satisfied with the US-Cuba relationship, however. One of those people who were dissatisfied was Fidel Castro. Since the 1959 revolution, the Cuban exodus can be divided into five main stages: the "Historical Exiles" (1959–62); the Freedom Flights (1965–73); the Mariel boatlift (1980); the *balsero* (rafter) crisis (1994); and the post-Soviet exodus (1995–2017). 2021–2024 is seeing a new wave.

FIDEL'S REVOLUTION

Many Cubans saw Castro as a powerful leader who would restore their national pride. Opposition to Batista was reportedly widespread. As Powell (2022) wrote, Bacardi President José "Pepin" Bosch helped fund the revolution, as did sugar broker Julio Lobo, who reportedly said "We didn't care who overthrew Batista as long as somebody did" (in Powell, 2022, p. 38). In 1959, he paraded his guerillas proudly through Havana. Compared to Batista, Castro seemed "fearless and incorruptible." Americans were initially under the Castro spell as well. Born in 1926, Castro's father Angel was a self-made man who owned a sugar factory. He sold it to the United Fruit Company, an American company. He had an affair with Lina Ruz Gonzalez, the result of which was Castro's birth, They married and did well, sending Fidel to a prestigious Jesuit school. The Jesuit priests were very conservative, and Castro was known to read works by Mussolini and Hitler. Not a fascist, though, historians say Castro was inspired by Mussolini's speeches and techniques. Having grown up in the sugar industry and being influenced by these speeches and writing, Castro was convinced that Cuba had and continued to suffer under American exploitation. He was very nationalistic and vowed to rid the island of American influence. The University of Havana, which Castro attended, was a hotbed of activism opposing American exploitation. Since the United States backed Batista, Castro naturally did not. As part of a student delegation Castro went to Colombia and got wrapped up in a violent insurrection. He saw the allure of violence as a political strategy. He was involved in a failed effort that landed many others jailed or killed. His trial helped make him a national celebrity. His prison sentence was 15 years, but he only served 19 months before being released in a general amnesty. As he emerged, the country was even more ripe for revolution than ever. He took to the mountains and waged guerilla warfare on Batista and his men. Castro used radio and mimeographs to spread his ideology, making his voice familiar across the island. He and his men were seen as Robin Hoods and Batista and his regime as the ruthless Sheriff of Nottingham. Argentinian doctor Che Guevara was one of Castro's followers. By the end of 1958, fighting had spread to the cities. Batista fled and Castro prepared to occupy Havana. Castro went to Washington in 1959, presenting himself as a dedicated Democrat. Back in Havana, however, he began to display authoritarianism. He went after Batista's henchmen, most of whom were not given fair trials. Some 600 were put to death by firing squad. He started nationalizing American businesses within months, including the United Fruit Company. Castro also had talks with the Soviet Union, ensuring it would be an ally to Cuba (PBS Frontline, 1992).

The United States responded by training guerillas and saboteurs to disrupt Castro's efforts. As Eckstein (2022) noted, "Washington resented and resisted Castro's rule because his revolution-in-the-making both undermined US business interests in Cuba and challenged US hegemony over Latin America and, to a lesser extent, other Third World countries" (p. 2). Just months after Castro took power, Richard Nixon, President Eisenhower's Vice President, proposed a plan to train anti-Castro Cuban exiles to form a guerilla force, a plan many exiles fully supported (Eckstein, 2022). The CIA also had a plan, A Program of Covert Action Against the Castro Regime," which was an effort to overthrow Cuba's leader and was authorized and funded (although minimally, at $4.4 million). It was to be covert because previous CIA-led coups had given the United States a bad name. The idea was to train anti-Castro exiles to infiltrate Cuba, help arrange defections, gather intelligence, and if needed, engage in guerilla warfare. The efforts were overseen by a Special Group called the 5412 Committee. By late summer of 1960, the CIA felt that the exiles training was not going well so arranged for the Army Special Forces to enhance their training in tactical assault. No US military was to be used in these attack efforts, as that would have violated international law and been perceived as an act of war, so instead the exiles that were being trained were to engage in actions that would trigger an uprising, thereby toppling the Castro regime. President Kennedy continued and expanded these covert efforts when he took office in January1961, nearly tripling the number of exiles receiving guerilla warfare training (Eckstein, 2022).

The most well-known of these attacks was the Bay of Pigs invasion. A trained guerilla squad of 1,500 exiles, called Brigade 2506, was to invade the island on April 17, 1961. Allegedly a secret, American involvement was obvious immediately. The CIA blundered desperately with the Bay of Pigs, playing right into Castro's hands. His victory in just days over the guerillas made him a hero to much of Cuba and to some of the rest of the world. Some 100 exiles were killed and almost 1200 members of Brigade 2506 were taken as prisoners of war (Eckstein, 2022). Eckstein (2022) explained, "the invasion contributed to the consolidation, as well as radicalization, of the revolution" (p. 17). He declared Cuba to be socialist and claimed that it was US aggression that pushed him to become more radical and to ally with the Soviets. He used the threat of a foreign enemy to build nationalist vigor. The failed invasion also demoralized opponents of Castro. It was also a costly mess, with the CIA spending $23 million just on the training of the exiles—far more than the budgeted $4.4 million (Eckstein, 2022). Nonetheless, the CIA did not give up on encouraging exiles to oust Castro. The next effort was to support them in sabotage, underground activity, and covert intelligence . One such effort that the Kennedy administration launched in November 1961 was called Operation Mongoose, which involved sending exiles to the island to release propaganda that would undermine the economy and supposedly turn Cubans against Castro. They also planned to blow up strategic targets in Cuba as well as to destroy crops (Eckstein, 2022).

Most people thought Castro would avoid the Soviet style of communism, rather people thought Castro would bring Marxism with a human face. Initially, the island saw a flourishing of arts and culture. Castro supporters brought literacy to remote villages. He created policies allowing everyone on the island access to education and to medical care, housing, and food. Parker (2017) explained that

> Throughout the 1960s, Cuba flourished, as Fidel Castro focused on reducing the overall illiteracy rate among Cuban citizens, by providing free education for all (K–12 through college), and implementing social programs that would benefit families....Cuba "has achieved far more social justice, and improved every social indicator far beyond the accomplishments of their own (often larger and richer) countries. Both first-hand observations and United Nations data verify these evaluations (in Farber, 2017, p. 9).

The island saw rapid growth in the number of lawyers, teachers, engineers, and doctors, as well as vocational and trade positions because those programs were also free. Prior to the revolution, healthcare was something only the wealthy could afford. Castro's regime established hospitals and clinics in the countryside and in small cities outside of Havana (Parker, 2017). The Urban Reform Law, enacted in March 1959, instituted lower rent prices for Cuban citizens and discouraged land grabs by wealthy Cubans. Specifically, it declared a 50 percent reduction in rents under $100 monthly, 40 percent reduction of those between $100 and $200 monthly, and 30 percent reduction in rent over $200 monthly. Further, the National Savings and Housing Institute (INAV0 took vacant property owned by wealth Cubans and turned it into low-cost public housing for lower- and middle-class families. The Agrarian Reform Law, enacted in May 1959, controlled the acreage citizens were allowed to own and maintain. Such reforms finally made dream of owning property reality, not just for a certain population based upon status, but for all Cubans who were willing to work hard on their own land. The previous notion of privatization of agriculture was replaced by the right of the local citizens to work on their own land. Additionally, the once-private beaches that were exclusive to the affluent were made free and open to everyone (Parker, 2017). In a May 1, 1960, speech entitled, "This is Democracy," Castro expressed how important Afro-Cubans and women were to Cuban society as a whole. He stated, "Democracy is this, where you, Black Cuban, have the right to work without anyone being able to deprive you of that right because of stupid prejudice. Democracy is this, where the women acquire rights equal to those of all other citizens and have a right even to bear arms alongside the men to defend their country" (Parker, 2017, p. 53).

Further, although he later declared Cuba to be an atheist country, Castro allowed all five synagogues continued to function, albeit with much reduced membership as many fled the island. Further, while radio broadcasts of religious services and religious publications were prohibited, weekly half hour radio talk shows in Yiddish were permitted. The state even took care of the Jewish cemeteries, and until 1975 the government bused Jewish children to their religious schools (Franklin, 2016). According to Levine (1993, p. 251), "Castro bent over backward not to persecute the Jews." The only private enterprises not to be nationalized were Jewish butchers and families who wanted to keep kosher were given different rations of meat and poultry. Kaplan (2001) reported that no property was taken and Jewish religious buildings, community centers, and cemeteries were all offered maintenance by the state.

It was only decades later that poverty and hunger became significant problems. The United States contributed to those problems, however, imposing a decades-long trade embargo on the island. Castro ordered farm production to grow by 15 percent a year for twelve years. This ambition plan was to be achieved by plowing land across the island to plant crops. In doing so, they demolished a lot of the habitat of the island. He also announced that he wanted to double the production of sugar, Cuba's biggest cash crop. This meant the entire economy revolved around sugar, which proved to be disastrous. This was the first of many failures. Further, anyone considered to be a counterrevolutionary was arrested and imprisoned. His regime also targeted gay people, as discussed in greater detail in Chapter 7 (PBS Frontline, 1992). Further, in the US President Dwight D. Eisenhower authorized an anti-Castro propaganda campaign in March 1960 designed to overthrow Castro. It included termination of sugar purchases, the end of oil deliveries, continuation of an arms embargo that had been launched in mid-1958, and the preparation of Cuban exiles to invade the island. Many Cuban Jews were upset to see the deteriorating relationship between the two countries. They worried that it would limit their access to materials and markets for their businesses. They were also worried that the US actions would cause Cuba to retaliate and institute even harsher economic measures. At the time, many congregations were completing building projects and they worried that the Cuban government would appropriate them for their own purposes. Jews were especially concerned that the Patronato would be confiscated, and small groups continued to go there to ensure that it appeared to be in use (Kaplan, 2005).

JEWISH EXODUS FROM CUBA

Few Cubans immigrated to the US before the revolution. This is due to immigration policy, which at the time strongly favored Europeans. Those who had the means had little reason to leave, as the middle and upper classes tended to be tight knit, with strong family ties and access to a life of luxury in a country referred to as Las Vegas before Las Vegas became big. They socialized together with others of the same race and social class in exclusive clubs and married people from similar backgrounds. Eckstein (2009) wrote that one of the clubs was so exclusive that Batista was refused admission on the count that he was of mixed blood and a laborer's son

Enrique recalled that after the revolution, kids started disappearing from his school. While he noted the difficulty of large businesses being nationalized, small businesses being driven to bankruptcy, people being thrown in jail and newspapers being taken over, he said the worst thing was not being able to trust neighbors anymore. On each block committees were formed to spy on would be counterrevolutionaries. He recalls people leaving in the middle of the night, not even saying goodbye. He remembers his class attendance in high school going from thirty-five students to three by 1961. The family tried to keep their dress factory open, but it was difficult to get materials to work with. By 1962, he said, "the government had become the supplier, the customer, the banker, the landlord, the overseer, etc." Even after the family left Cuba Eva dreamed that she would be able to return and again run Modas Ethel.

While the advances described above sound to me to be amazing, they were not well-received by most of the middle-and upper-class Jews. The first to leave Cuba after the revolution were military officers, government officials, landowners, and businesspersons, many of whom were associated with the Batista regime. Many of Cuba's Jews were among the earliest to leave, with a sizable portion landing in Miami, for several obvious reasons. These exiles have also been referred to as "Golden Exiles," as most came from the upper and middle classes. They were generally urban, educated, white-skinned, and professionals. Powell (2022) reported that 94 percent of those who left in the earliest days were White. As Bettinger-López (2000) noted,

> Cuba (especially Havana) in 1959 was filled with elites, many of whom had achieved socioeconomic success through connections with the United States, ownership of large land tracts and private businesses in Cuba, and intimacy with the Batista regime. The revolutionary regime's initial goals thus posed imminent political and economic dangers for these elites. Their ties with the capitalist America made them revolutionary targets, and their migration was spurred by the Castro government's nationalization of private businesses and American industry, its implementation of agrarian reform laws, and the United States government's increasingly strained political and economic ties with Cuba (p. 9).

Behar (2021) explained

> The Yiddish-speaking Jews who arrived from Poland in the 1920s were among the founders of the Communist Party and had needed Yiddish translators, they were so fresh off the boat, but by the early 1960s, most had prospered and aligned themselves with the capitalist world. In turn, the Ladino-speaking Sephardic Jews from Turkey felt echoes of the expulsion from Spain centuries earlier. Jews of both traditions did not want to be part of a new world where food would be rationed, their children would go to school with children of all races, social classes and religious backgrounds, and Jewish holidays would need to be celebrated secretly. And so,

they started anew in the United States, mostly going to Miami along with the rest of the 200,000 Cuban immigrants who recreated a nostalgic vision of their lost island home and developed a consciousness of themselves as exiles who would one day go back to a free Cuba (p. 161).

In addition to confiscating properties and taking over business, there were other very scary things happening that prompted the exodus that included this family. Castro's people were rounding up and executing by firing squad supporters of Batista (Powell, 2022) and encouraged people to spy on their neighbors, which Enrique mentioned.

The United States government admitted 248,100 Cuban immigrants between 1959 and 1962, with some 14,000 minors admitted between December 1960 and October 1962 in what is known as Operation Pedro Pan. Things might have gotten difficult when, on January 3, 1961, the US broke diplomatic relations with Cuba, but it extended benefits to Cuban migrants in the form of visa waivers. Upon arriving to the US, Cubans could be paroled or gain refugee status, claiming they were fleeing communist oppression. Although previous migrations of Jews were due in large part to discrimination and persecution, Kaplan argues that the migration from Cuba after the Castro revolution was not due to antisemitism. She asserts that it was the result of political and economic changes, while Steinberg (N.D.) asserts that the migration was mostly due to economics. She maintains that. "Had free-market enterprise remained intact, the Jewish middle class would have entered alternative foreign markets to sustain their businesses. Since this was not the case, Jews were more affected by Castro's attempt to redistribute wealth in Cuba through the nationalization of industry" (p. 3). Fidel Castro was said to have been shocked by the Jewish exodus. He reportedly exclaimed, "Why are the Jews leaving? We have nothing against them" (Behar, 2021, p. 161). Upset at the exodus not just of Jews but many other Cubans, Castro referred to them as "*gusanos*" (worms) and "*escoria*" (trash) (American Experience, 2005). Others also taunted the people who were trying to leave Cuba using those terms as well as calling them traitors (Powell, 2022).

Before the exodus from Cuba there was a small community of American Jews that were already in South Florida. The first wave of American Jews to South Florida began in the 1920s and lasted until about the mid-1950s. It was largely comprised of Jews from the Northeast United States and helped develop an economic boom in the South Beach area. Proximity to Cuba and a similar climate helped usher in a second wave, which occurred in the 1960s when approximately 5,000 Cuban Jews sought refuge in South Florida after Fidel Castro came to power (Bettinger-López, 2000).

Lilia and Jack were the first to leave after the revolution. Her family was concerned about things they heard could be possible with kids being sent to labor camps and were dealing with the uncertainty of their business and livelihood. Rumors were circulating that the regime was sending girls into the rural areas to help in its literacy campaigns and that they would be assaulted by men there. They wanted to send her to the US to keep her safe and had prepared her paperwork to travel to Maryland to live with a relative. Just 16 years old, she and Jack had been dating somewhat seriously. When he learned that they planned to send her away, he said he wanted to go with her. He proposed and they had approximately two months to plan their wedding. They got married at the Patronato on November 13, 1960. They were not able to be married by a rabbi, as all had already left Cuba. They had a few days of honeymoon in the beautiful beach resort town of Verdado, then left Cuba on November 27, 1960, never to return. She emphasizes that she was "a little girl." This was just nine months after Castro had been sworn in as Prime Minister. After they were processed in Miami, they ended up in Kansas City, where Jack's sister Sarita and her husband Barney were living. This was a total culture shock! Neither knew much English, but they set about trying to learn and getting jobs. Barney tried to "Americanize" Jack. It was he that suggested he go by Jack instead of Isaac/Itzaak. He worked as an insurance salesperson, something the reserved man was ill-suited for. After not too long they moved to Los Angeles, where Aunt Mania and Uncle Louis were living, and he ran a liquor store.

IMAGE 2.1.   The Patronato, from July 2023.
Site of Lilia and Jack's wedding in 1960

IMAGE 2.2   Lilia and Jack's wedding, 1960

IMAGE 2.3.   From left to right, Isaac, Consuelo, Lilia, Jack,
Eva, and David at Lilia and Jack's wedding

IMAGE 2.4.   Lilia and Enrique at her wedding

Lilia's parents Consuelo and Isaac left Cuba thereafter, and reportedly Isaac swallowed a diamond so he could have some capital when he arrived in the United States. No one is clear on what happened with it, exactly. The story is that everyone left with nothing, but it is possible there is more to it than that. Lilia does not know, but her parents' passports show that they traveled to and from Miami in August 1961, a few months before she and Jack left. It is possible that, as a businessman, Isaac was able to establish something that would help them financially. They ended up in New York and opened a jewelry store that eventually employed both grandmothers as well as Lilia and Jack. Lilia does not really recall much about the process of actually leaving Cuba and arriving in the US, other than their immigration was processed in Miami. She was not aware of the special visa program offered to Cubans at the time. Those born in Cuba, and the parents of children born in Cuba, were eligible for a visa waiver allowing for them to enter the US as essentially economic refugees (Kaplan, 2005). This is discussed in greater detail in Chapter 6. The grandchildren of exiles that I interviewed all believed that their grandparents fled Cuba due to the oppression of communism. They seemed to believe this would impact their grandparents' ability to worship. Both Dylan and Rachel B. made this point. In reality, this does not seem to have been the case. It was more of an economic decision. I found this to be interesting.

As will be clear in subsequent chapters, the narrative seems to be that they were victims of the Castro regime and had to flee under dangerous and chaotic conditions, like refugees. In Chapter 6, I show how the US government reinforced that narrative in its immigration policy and aid to Cuban exiles.

Eva, David, and Enrique left Cuba on April 30, 1961. Enrique recalls much more about the leaving process. They had quite the adventure! They had waited Iine at the American embassy and were finally able to get tourist visas to the US based on David's health and the need to see specialists. This was to allow them to leave Cuba temporarily. They were supposed to leave on April 17 . That was the day of the Bay of Pigs Invasion. The failed attempt resulted in the closure of the airport, so when they got there the family was turned away. This was not only disappointing but scary, as most people left secretly so they risked being outed as counterrevolutionaries. Furthermore, they knew they only had a few more weeks to secure mew flights as Eva's visa was set to expire. With the help of friends, they were able to get new flight reservations for April 27. While they waited at the gate, an announcement on the loudspeaker declared that taking money out of the country was prohibited. Each person was only allowed to take $3 dollars with them, and agents were set up at the airport to review each passenger's possessions. Enrique, David, and Eva each had theirs in dimes. He and David went to the table at the gate and declared what they had. Eva tried to explain that they would need some money upon arriving in Miami and he thought she was discussing what had previously been declared, so said to her, "lady, just sit down." She did, assuming that meant that her $3 in dimes was already acknowledged and accepted. As the plane loaded single file, David got on first. Enrique walked with his mother, and she was asked to open her purse. They found her dimes and she tried to explain what happened, but the authorities did not care. They got a mortified David off of the plane and sent the whole family to the other side of the airport, where their baggage was searched. Eva had bought several shirts as gifts, and these were interpreted as contraband. Their passports were suspended, they were all strip-searched by Cuba's G-2 (secret police), and their baggage confiscated. A trial date was to be set for several months later they were told. As he saw the plane, they were supposed to be on departing David had what may have been a mild heart attack. They stayed at an airport hotel and a doctor declared him fine, but the family was embarrassed to go home. They were saved by Issac and Consuelo Schigiel, Lilia's parents, who had contacts that could help them. Two days later their trial for having contraband was suspended and their passports were returned. Their baggage was not, but still they considered this a miracle. They had to leave on April 30, as May 1 was a federal holiday for International labor Day and the airport was closed, and Eva's visa was to expire on May 2. A cousin's husband at the airport used Enique's Bar Mitzvah watch to grease the wheels and get them actually on the plane.

They first tried to settle in Los Angeles but decided fairly quickly that Miami was the best place for them. Enrique's path to the US involved being separated from his parents for approximately 18 months. He stayed with his sister in Kansas

City for a summer and then with an aunt in Los Angeles. His parents and brother moved around from Los Angeles to New York and then to Miami, where they all reunited in 1962. His father had limited capacity to work due to his health issues, but Eva got a job in a shoe factory in Hialeah. They had spent a lot of time looking at small businesses for sale but had little capital since they left Cuba with only their baggage. Enrique recalls her rising at 4 am and taking two or three buses to make it to work by 7 am. She held that job, where she made $1 per hour, for two years. He also worked at a shoe store for approximately 30 hours per week while also going to school full time. David stayed home and tried to help by making lunch and dinner and doing other chores around the house. He also helped Enrique with his English homework, giving him a verbal synopsis of the books he was to read. David learned English very quickly and Enrique said he was in awe of that. At home they kept kosher, as his parents were quite religious, but his father "cheated" in non-kosher restaurants when Eva was not around. David passed away in 1964 from a heart attack. Enrique says he lost both his father and his best friend. Jack and Lilia's father Isaac invited Eva to join them in New York and work in the jewelry business they had started. At 59, Enrique said he is unsure what else she would have done and is grateful that they gave her the opportunity. She also suffered from crippling arthritis and her English was not great. Eva worked for the business for more than 30 years. Her special talent was in designing and laying out the display window each morning. Jack drove her to and from work each day until they all moved to Miami and opened two stores as Sunshine Jewelry. More on this in subsequent chapters.

Ester and Rachel were children when they left Cuba. They don't have strong memories of it, more just impressions of food and climate. Both said they struggled with learning English and were often made fun of for mangling words. Ester, who is a retired college professor, reflected on the family's plight and its continued impact on her life. "Our family's flight from Cuba to the United States was an extension of its ancestral Jewish struggle for freedom from political and religious persecution. Intimately familiar with the Bolshevik revolution which had destroyed my paternal grandfather's Jewish bourgeois family, my kin were alert to the first sounds of Marxist rhetoric" (p. 88). They left Havana when she was just eight, in October 1960. She and her siblings believed they were going on a vacation to Miami, as that is what their parents told them. She explains, however, that "My parents; words—that we were taking our usual Miami vacation—were belied by the air of barely suppressed panic and the thoroughness of our packing. One indelible image captured the contradictions of my new life and divided consciousness: my parents; open clothes closet, totally empty except for a row of still little-girl's petticoats, useless and decorative" (p. 89). She recalls stopping at Consuelo's home on the way to the airport, where everyone was loaded with all the gold jewelry they could possibly wear without arousing suspicion. They stayed at the Tropics hotel, and she remembers being devastated when her parents told her that these items were not gifts but rather belonged to Tia Consuelo, who needed them back (Rok, 1995). It was approximately one month into their "vacation" in a conversation about Castro that Ester stood corrected about the true nature of their exodus. She spoke of Castro in heroic, reverential terms, as the family still did, when Edith retorted, 'You are wrong, Ester Rebeca, Castro is bad, es malo, it is because of him that we have left Cuba, and can never go back" (Rok, 1995, p. 89). Yet she also notes that leaving Cuba was considered "mild" in comparison to her parents' departure from Eastern Europe. "In our family psyche, leaving and losing Cuba was unremarkable in the many lifetimes of diaspora, moving like Gypsies wherever we might not be punished for being ourselves. On the rare occasions in my childhood when I mentioned to my family my profound sense of loss, of intense curiosity and deep longing for Cuba, they would inevitably reply: you don't have any idea how easy you had it as an immigrant, compared to what we endured in leaving Russia and Poland" (Rok, 1995, pp. 90–981).

Most Jewbans, like Ester, expected to go home. They did, however, often hide important personal items in their clothing or suitcases just in case. This included school transcripts, marriage certificates, jewelry and more, just as Isaac reportedly swallowed a diamond (Perez, 2013). Interestingly, Kaplan (2005) reported that the redistribution of wealth promoted by the government's early measures stimulated retail purchases, and many of these small stores were able to significantly increase sales and reduce the existing stock. This in turn enabled these families to pay for their emigration and even buy dollars to take with them to the United States.6 But by the time some of them tried to do this, greater restrictions were in place, and some found their dollars confiscated and in some cases their immigration blocked entirely" (p. 134). Further, as Eckstein (2009) noted, "Despite their definition of themselves as exiles, only a small number of them had actually suffered for their political convictions"(pp. 14–15).

Not all families left in the way that Lilia and Jack's family did. Some were separated and left as part of what became known as Operation Pedro Pan. This initiative started in 1961 and brought 14,048 children to the US without their parents. 396 of those kids were Jewish. Marcos Kerbel was one of them. His parents had a thriving clothing store they were hesitant to leave in hopes that the revolution would not be long-lasting. Kerbel was processed through the Miami HIAS Office but then sent to Los Angeles the same day to live in a Jewish orphanage. He was then sent to live with a strictly Orthodox family, which he found difficult before his uncles arrived from Cuba to Miami in June 1962 and then his parents on October 19, on the next-to-last Pan Am flight before the Cuban Missile Crisis stopped all flights from Cuba to the US until 1965 (Kaplan, 2005). He knew Enrique from Jewish school in Cuba.

As noted above, the Bay of Pigs was a huge fiasco and rather than unseating Castro, it served to rally many Cubans and Cuban allies around the world. It also resulted in deep distrust of the Kennedy administration among many Jews. This distrust of Democrats can still be seen among many Cubans in the US. Reportedly some of the soldiers who took part in the failed CIA-sponsored invasion were

Jews whose parents had arrived in Cuba after fleeing Nazi persecution. Many were among the prisoners the Castro regime rounded up after the attack (Dolsten, 2016). While Castro was generally good to the Jews living on the island, he was an outspoken critic of Israel. In 1979 he spoke about Israeli war crimes against Palestinians at the UN General Assembly (Dolsten, 2016). Unlike Perez (2013), only two of my interviewees, Marcos, and Enrique, mentioned the Bay of Pigs at all, let alone had strong feelings on how it was handled. Neither were overtly critical; rather, they mentioned it as a marker in regard to when they left Cuba. Perhaps this lack of attention to the fiasco is because most of the exiles I interviewed had already left Cuba. Perhaps also because they were so vehemently anti-Castro, even a botched attempt to overthrow him did not bother these exiles and their children and grandchildren.

It was the Cuban Missile Crisis in the fall of 1962 that closed Cuba's doors for those seeking to leave until the Carioca boatlift and then the Freedom Flights that ran from 1965–1973. The Missile Crisis was a time of tremendous fear in the US and in Cuba, as the US and the Soviet Union were at the brink of a nuclear conflict. In July 1962, Soviet premier Nikita Khrushchev reached a secret deal with Castro to allow Soviet nuclear missiles to be placed on the island. Construction of several missile sites began before US intelligence found out about the buildup of Soviet weapons. On September 4, 1962, President John F. Kennedy issued a warning to Cuba and the Soviet Union, declaring that these moves were perceived as an offensive. Despite the warning US surveillance found the buildup continued, prompting Kennedy to summon his closest advisors and consider options. Some wanted an air strike to destroy the missiles then an invasion of Cuba, others wanted to continue with stern warnings to both Cuba and the Soviet Union. On October 22, Kennedy decided on a naval quarantine of Cuba. He also sent a letter to Krushchev demanding that the weapons be dismantled and removed to the Soviet Union. The two exchanged many direct and indirect communications throughout the crisis. Kennedy announced on public television, "It shall be the policy of this nation to regard any nuclear missile launched from Cuba against any nation in the Western Hemisphere as an attack by the Soviet Union on the United States, requiring a full retaliatory response upon the Soviet Union." Krushchev responded that the quarantine was actually a blockage and thus an act of war. As the Soviets continued to build their nuclear weapons, which were near operational readiness in Cuba, Kennedy determined to give diplomatic efforts one last try while also readying American forces at DEFCON 2, meaning preparing for war. After additional exchanges the crisis ended on October 28, when Krushchev agreed to dismantle and remove the missiles from Cuba and Kennedy agreed to end the quarantine, not to invade Cuba, and later to remove US Jupiter missiles from Turkey (Office of the Historian, N.D.). By the end of the crisis, "almost no one now believed that Castro would soon fall from power. Those Cuban Jews who had waited in the country hoping that Castro would soon fall now made plans to emigrate" (Kaplan, 2005, p. 137).

RECEPTION OF JEWS AND JEWBANS IN THE US

The first wave of Jewish immigrants to South Florida had to establish their own community. They did so slowly, at first. The first recorded circumcision in Miami was in 1907, and in 1913 there was a Jewish wedding on Miami Beach. The first Jewish congregation, which became Beth David, was established in 1913 after the death of a Jewish tourist. By 1915 there were at least 55 Jews in Miami, with the population growing to 3,500 by the 1920s due to the developing infrastructure, automobile and commercial aviation, abundant land, and promotion for travel and real estate. When the second wave arrived, they were not necessarily welcoming, viewing them as intruders and freeloaders. Eventually, however, members of the second wave were able to integrate somewhat into the Jewish community. "While the immigration from Cuba was surely traumatic for many, religion appeared to be a uniting factor for the Jewish Cuban community, as they lived together in the same areas, established their own institutions, and eventually integrated into the existing institutions. Furthermore, the authors claim that religion acts as the most principal factor in the "development of ethnic communities and the reassertion of national cultures" (Portes & Rumbaut, 2006, p. 304). The Jewbans did, however, develop many of their own institutions, religious and otherwise, and did so with an eye for reproducing their lives in Cuba.

Antisemitism was rampant in South Florida at the time. The Ku Klux Klan was active in the 1920s and 1930s, and Jews and Blacks were banned from public beaches. Hotels advertised jobs with signs reading "Gentiles only need apply." Signs saying, "No Jews or Dogs" were also common, while an advertisement for a Miami Beach oceanfront hotel read "Always a view, never a Jew" (Levine, 2023). These restrictions shaped where Jews could live and work (Sheskin, 1993, p. 125). For instance, influential developers, including Highway builder and Entrepreneur Carl G. Fisher's, refused to serve Jewish customers. Oil and Railroad Mogul Henry Flagler (1830–1913) prohibited land sales and hotel lodgings to Jewish clients (Levine, 2023). This antisemitism is due perhaps in part to the fact that Florida did not allow Jews to settle until 1763 and was one of the last cities to develop a substantial Jewish population. Over time, Jews made significant contributions to Miami's growing economy. They were involved in the hotel, banking, and construction industries. As the struct limits of Jewish ownership of real estate on Miami Beach were repealed in the 1930s, it became a hub for Jewish activity. Many real estate owners still had a large amount of debt on their properties from the Great Depression, so they were eager to sell it to Jews, even if they were still antisemitic. Jewish developers started to build hotels on Collins Avenue and Ocean Drive in Miami Beach, helping to create the now-famous Art Deco district. The first wave also established the Jewish Community Service of Greater Miami, which offered refugee resettlement assistance, foster care and adoption services, and mental health assistance to the Jewish community (Moore, 2023).

In the 1930s and 1940s, Miami became a training place for military recruits. The Army Air Corps leased Miami Beach Municipal Golf Course for just one dollar per year. It was used as a training school and drill grounds. Over time, the Army appropriated 85 percent of the hotels in Miami Beach, many built by Jews, using them to house soldiers. Restaurants were turned into mess halls and Miami Beach became essentially an army base. Many of the recruits were Jews who returned to live in Miami after World War II. The hotels were returned to their pre-war owners and businesses on Miami Beach continued to thrive post-war. By the mid-1940s, the Miami-Dade area was home to more than 30,000 Jews, with about half of them living on Miami Beach (Moore, 2023). The growth in industry in Miami also included Jewish organizations and institutions. This included the Jewish Federation of Miami in 1938 and the Jewish Home for the Aged in 1940. In 1944 the Bureau of Jewish Education of Greater Miami was founded to foster the study of Judaism and its traditions, culture, values, and heritage. There were eight synagogues in Miami by 1944, as well as the organizations B'nai B'rith, American Jewish Congress, National Council of Jewish Women, Hadassah, the YMCA, Jewish Social Service Bureau, and the Greater Miami Jewish Federation. A group of Sephardic Jews formed the Sephardic Brotherhood of Greater Miami and a synagogue in the 1940s. In 1945 the Anti-Defamation League spearheaded an effort to remove the "gentiles only" signs in Miami Beach, and Jewish leaders implored the Miami Beach City Council to prohibit antisemitic advertising because it discouraged Jewish visitors. It did so in 1947 but the law was overturned by the courts. The state legislature gave the Council the right to ban discriminatory advertising in 1949. By 1947, there were twenty-four congregations. By 1950 it had been combined with the Sephardic Jewish Brotherhood of America Branch in Miami and renamed the Sephardic Jewish Center of Greater Miami. Yet despite all of these services, the rapid influx of Jewish migrants resulted in some disorganization, and many had brought with them a "permanent tourist" mentality. Thus, there was no unified Jewish community (Moore, 2023).

Between 1950 and 1955, approximately 650 Jews arrived in Miami every month. The Jewish population grew 300 percent, to 55,000 in Miami-Dade. Only four percent of the Jewish population had been born in Miami, so the vast majority were migrants, mostly from the North. A new home was built every seven minutes, with many of the builders Jews. It was again a huge explosion of people moving to Miami, and Jews were a significant part of it. They contributed to the economic, social, and cultural life, and soon, the political life of Miami Dade County. In 1952, Abe Aranovitz was the first Jewish mayor of Miami (Moore, 2023). As more migrants came to Miami, many Jews moved from Miami Beach to North Miami and North Miami Beach. Miami came to be known as "The Southern Borscht Belt," with many saying it was essentially a suburb of New York City (Moore, 2023).

Some reports indicated that the Cuban Jews who came immediately after the revolution were not welcomed by the first wave and that they had to create their own institutions. Bettinger-López (2000) was told that the Jewbans received little financial assistance nor moral support. Rabbi Meyer Abramowitz, who was one of the only rabbis to welcome the Jewbans to his synagogue, Temple Menorah, many American Jews assumed that "Cuban Jews were wealthy and so did not need economic or social assistance" (Bettinger-López, 2000, p. 23). There was a general perception that the Jewbans were educated professionals who could bring with them their fortunes. Clearly, this was not the truth, as most were unable to bring more than a few pieces of luggage (Bettinger-López, 2000). Further, most in Miami held anti-Cuban sentiments, with restaurants featuring signs reading "No Pets, No Kids, No Cubans" (Rich, 1996. p. 148). As their parents before them in Cuba, most Jewbans who emigrated had to take menial, low-paying jobs, even those who had been professionals on the island. Enrique commented on the ways American Jews received Cuba Jews in Miami. He e recalls that the American Jews drove fancy cars while the Cuban Jews rode the bus. Many major stars were involved in making Miami a less-than-welcoming place for Cubans.

Jack had been studying engineering in Cuba but was unable to finish, as the University of Havana was often shut down due to protests. Despite being educated, as noted above he was only able to work with his brother-in-law selling insurance when they first arrived in Kansas City. Not knowing much English and having a reserved personality made that difficult. Lilia secured a job with Hallmark cards and made more than Jack did, which was quite unusual at the time. Also, like their parents before them, they found a society vastly different from the one they knew. It was cold in late November, and they lacked appropriate clothes. Lilia also described the segregation that bothered her, as it seemed so different from her experience in Cuba. She recalls using a water fountain and being yelled at by a woman who told her she had to wait in line to use the water fountain for Whites, not the one for people of color that had no line. She also recalls how her accent was misunderstood in a comical story about going to shop for bed sheets. Her accent made it sound like she was asking for "shits," and when the salesperson seemed appalled she had no idea what the problem was! Although life was not easy, they had it better than many immigrants, as they had family who offered them help. Enrique recalls One help service was El Refuge, but only those who were desperate went there. He also recalls assistance from HIAS. Lilia did not recall any assistance that they received outside of that of Sarita and Barney and a little from HIAS. Although it is not really part of the family narrative, they also benefited from many other services and policies specific to Cubans. This is addressed in more detail in Chapter 8. Although it was much later, Enrique and Helen lived in Rockford, IL, near Skokie, a town infamous for a Nazi parade in the later 1997. He said they witnessed lots of antisemitism there. Their kids were the only non-Blondes and the only Jews at their school.

Like in Cuba, the Ashkenazi and Sephardic communities were largely separated. Younger people often mixed together but the older generations rarely did. The Sephardic Jewish immigrants from Cuba had an even rougher time than did the Ashkenazi, whose light skin and religious practices made them less distinct from the existing Jewish community. The Sephardic, in contrast, were easily distinguishable because of their "olive complexion, their volatility, emotionally and otherwise, and their strong adherence to tradition" (Liebman, 1969, p. 243). They typically lived in separate areas so as to continue their lifestyle and customs (Bettinger-López, 2000).

Like most other Cubans in the US and the Jewbans in particular, Cubans in South Florida are far lighter skinned than is representative of the country. This is due to racial bias that resulted from the initial privileging of Cuban immigrants, who tended to be White as well as more financially able and have more connections for economic success. The continuation of those privileges over decades meant that those individuals could more easily bring over family members, who were also largely White. As Eckstein (2022) writes, "The first to take advantage of the US welcome mat were the light-skinned upper and middle classes, when the Castro-led government stripped them of their property and privilege and turned on opponents of the revolution's increasing radicalization" (p. 333). Later Cuban immigrants added racial diversity but came under vastly different circumstances and were not necessarily welcomed in cities like Miami by the existing Cubans, who sometimes judged the newcomers for not leaving earlier. Most of David's family does not look Cuban and, as is discussed in the next Chapter, do not really associate with Cuban immigrants, only fellow Jewbans. Rieff (1995) described it in harsher terms,

> Every diaspora judges itself, whether secretly or ostentatiously, to be both unique and uniquely sinned against. In this, the three quarters of a million Cuban Americans of South Florida are anything but exceptional. But like the Jews, the Armenians, and the White Russians before them, the Miami Cubans have tended to see themselves, both in their qualities and in their historical grievances, as sui generis. The common currency of exile is memory, above all the memory of wounds. But what may be necessary for group survival within the context of an exile group inevitably will appear to many outsiders, who share neither the memories nor the wounds, as touchy, clannish self-absorption. This has been the case with the Cuban exile community in South Florida in its relations with non-Cuban Miami, and, more broadly, with U.S. public opinion at large ever since Cuban refugees first started arriving in Miami after the victory of Fidel Castro in 1959.

Jewbans in South Florida longed to recreate what they had in Cuba. As Levine (2010) wrote, "Even those who left for the United States and who gained more material success in their new country always saw Cuba as the better place" (p. 247). Two of the most important places for Jews in Havana were the Guanabacoa Cemetery and the Casino Deportivo, a social club for Jews on the beach. One exile whom Bettinger-López interviewed asserted that the Cuban Jews made two big mistakes upon arrival in Miami—not buying enough plots in Mount Sinai Cemetery, which resulted in burials in many different locations, and not building a beach club. Others echoed those sentiments, heaping praise on the beautiful Casino Deportivo in Havana. It is described as a huge country club with all kinds of amenities, including bowling alleys, tennis courts, pools and more. This view of Cuba through rose-colored glasses is discussed in Chapter 7.

Exiles largely used Spanish in their everyday lives, so much so that in Miami, many Anglos who resented the exiles (for several reasons) mobilized to make English the official language. A 1980 campaign for English Only resulted in repeal of a Bilingual/Bicultural ordinance the city had passed in 1973, while another effort made it illegal to use county funds for activities not in English and for promoting any culture other than the US. In 1988, the English Only movement secured an amendment to the Florida constitution declaring English to be the official language (Eckstein, 2009). Later, the exiles also manipulated politics for their own anti-Castro actions. For example, in 1996 exiles convinced the Miami-Dade government to pass an ordinance preventing the use of funds for events involving Cuban artists.

Today, South Florida is home to some 650,000 Jews. It holds the largest concentration of Jews outside of Israel.

THE JEWS WHO STAYED IN CUBA

A small population of Jews stayed in Cuba after the exodus. Some were communists, others were hesitant to leave because they had become extremely attached to Cuba. Others were simply too elderly or too poor to leave (Kaplan, 2005). LaPorte, et al (2009) studied the Cuban Jews that remain in Havana, finding that although small, it is well organized. Respondents in their study said it was hard to practice their Judaism from the 1960s to the 1990s, even though it was not prohibited. One respondent stated, "My father was a revolutionary and died as a real Fidelista. In those days, being Jewish was a taboo. When looking for a job, if you indicated Jewish or Catholic, forget about it. So, they forgot about it (laughter)." Another responded similarly, saying, "It was not anti-Semitism, because the same happened to Catholics and to those of other faiths." Gallor (2022) commented,

> The Cuban Jews who remained after the revolution experienced a period when Jewish culture languished and religious life in general was subdued. Once again, despite its challenges, the community survived and became another example of the resilience and capacity of Jews in the Diaspora to adapt much like my parents and the countless Cubans who immigrated to the U.S. after the revolution adapted.

Today there are only approximately 1,200 Jews in Miami, with 1,000 in Havana and the remaining living in the countryside. *NPR* reported in May 2021 that there is not a single rabbi left on the island of Cuba. There are five synagogues in the country, with three of them located in Havana. These serve the estimated 1,200 people remaining in the country. The COVID pandemic hurt those synagogues even more, as they were relying heavily on tourists to attend services and make donations, but travel was stopped (Wisniewski, 2021). Jews outside of Havana struggle more to maintain their Jewish identity simply due to less access to Jewish community centers and services. As well, the tradition to marry intrareligious is difficult to maintain given the small number of Jews (Goldman, 1997). After the collapse of the Soviet Union in 1989, Cuba eased government controls on religion and in 1992, the Cuban constitution was modified making the country secular rather than atheist. This resulted in a surge of interest in Judaism. Further, respondents reported that Pope John Paul II's visit to the island in 1998 resulted in greater support for and interest in religion in. Fidel Castro also attended the Patronato's Hanukkah celebration that year, and later he began allowing Jews to emigrate to Israel(Laporte et al, 2009).

Since the 1990s, the American Jewish Joint Distribution (JDC) has helped run services, organize activities, and bring aid to Cuba. The American Jewish Federation helped fund renovations to the Patronato. In 1997 the organization B'Nai B'Rith formed a Committee on Cuban Affairs that brought food, clothes, and medicine to Cuba (Kaplan, 2001).

CONCLUSION

As this chapter has shown, the revolution may have been welcome in some ways but quickly Cubans, including the Jewbans, realized it would dramatically alter their lives. In contrast to rural Cubans who benefitted, at least in part, the Jewbans saw little benefit and quickly the majority left the island. Most never returned, and, as Chapter 7 discusses, have very little interest or awareness about Cuba today.

REFERENCES

American Experience. (2005). Cuban exiles in America. *PBS.* https://www.pbs.org/wgbh/americanexperience/features/castro-cuban-exiles-america/

Behar, R. (2021). The girl in the blue school uniform. Nashim: *A Journal of Jewish Women's Studies & Gender Issues, 39,* 159–165.

Bettinger-López, C. (2000). *Cuban-Jewish journeys: Searching for identity, home, and history in Miami.* University of Tennessee Press.

Dolsten, J. (2016). 7 moments that define Castros ties with Jews. *Times of Israel.* https://www.timesofisrael.com/7-moments-that-defined-castros-relationship-with-jews/

Eckstein, S. (2009). *The immigrant divide: How Cubans changes the US and their homeland.* Routledge.

Eckstein, S. (2022). *Cuban privilege: The making of immigrant inequality in America.* Cambridge University Press.

Farber, S. (2007). *The origins of the Cuban revolution reconsidered.* The University of North Carolina Press.

Farber, S. (2015. September). Cuba before the revolution. *Jacobin.* https://jacobin.com/2015/09/cuban-revolution-fidel-castro-casinos-batista4

Franklin, D. (2016). *The Jewish lived experience in Cuba.* Dissertation for The University of Alabama. https://ir-api.ua.edu/api/core/bitstreams/d86bf9a7-5c95-4424-9577-6032807c70b0/content

Gallor, S. (2022, December 23). Cuban American and Jewish: Exploring the history and intersection of my communities. *Reform Judaism.* https://reformjudaism.org/blog/cuban-american-and-jewish-exploring-history-and-intersections-my-communities

Goldman, I. (1997). Documentaries about Jewish renewal in contemporary Cuba: Hope or hype? *Latin American Research Review, 32*(3), 258–268.

Kaplan, D. (2001). *The Jews of Cuba since the Castro revolution.* American Jewish Year Book. https://www.bjpa.org/content/upload/bjpa/101c/101cuba.pdf

Kaplan, D. (2005). Fleeing the revolution: The exodus of Cuban Jewry in the early 1960s. *Cuban Studies, 36,* 129–155.

Laporte, H., Sweifach, J., & Strug, D. (2009). Jewish life in Cuba today. *Journal of Jewish Communal Service, 84*(3/4), 313–324.

Levine, M. (2023, February 19). The Jews of Florida: A history. *Aish.* https://aish.com/the-jews-of-florida-a-history/

Levine, R. (1993). *Tropical diaspora: The Jewish experience in Cuba.* University of Florida Press.

Levine, R. (2010). *Tropical diaspora: The Jewish experience in Cuba.* Markus Weiner Publishers.

Liebman, S. (1969). The Cuban Jewish community in South Florida. *American Jewish Yearbook, 70,* 238–246.

Moore, D. (2023). Miami Beach: The making of a Jewish resort city. *Jewish Culture and History, 24*(4), 453–469.

Office of the Historian. (n.d.). The Cuban Missile Crisis, October 1962. *United States Department of State.* https://history.state.gov/milestones/1961–1968/cuban-missile-crisis#:~:text=The%20Cuban%20Missile%20Crisis%20of,came%20closest%20to%20nuclear%20conflict.

PBS Frontline. (1992). *The last communist.* https://www.pbs.org/wgbh/frontline/documentary/the-last-communist/

Powell, D. (2022). *Ninety miles and a lifetime away: Memories of early Cuban exiles.* University of Florida Press.

Pérez, L. (2011). *Cuba: Between reform and revolution.* Oxford University Press.

Perez, R. (2013). Paradise lost: Older Cuban American exiles' ambiguous loss of leaving the homeland. *Journal of Gerontological Social Work, 56*(7), 596–622.

Perez, L. (2018). *Sugar, cigars, and revolution: The making of Cuban New York.* NYU Press.

Portes, A., & Rumbaut, R. (2006). *Immigrant America: A portrait* (3rd ed.). University of California Press.

Rich, W. (1996). *The politics of minority coalitions: Race, ethnicity, and shared uncertainties.* Praeger.

Rieff, D. (1995). From exiles to immigrants. *Foreign Affairs.* https://www.foreignaffairs.com/ru/articles/cuba/1995-07-01/exiles-immigrants

Rok, E. (1995). Finding what had been lost in plain view. In E. Behar (Ed.), *Bridges to Cuba/Puentes a Cuba* (pp. 85–985). University of Michigan Press.

Sheskin, I. (1993). Jewish metropolitan homelands. *Journal of Cultural Geography, 13*(2), 119–32.

Wisniewski, R. (2021, May 23). The youth of Cuba's tiny Jewish community. *NPR.* https://www.npr.org/sections/pictureshow/2021/05/23/988759260/the-youth-of-cubas-tiny-jewish-minority

PART 2

INTERVIEWS WITH THREE
GENERATIONS OF JEWBANS

CHAPTER 3

IDENTITY, FAMILY AND COMMUNITY AMONGST THE JEWBANS

One of the questions I asked all of the people I interviewed was the degree to which they identify as Cuba, Jewish, Jewban or all of the above. This produced some interesting findings, discussed herein. Eric Erikson, perhaps the father of the study of the formation of identity, noted the importance of adolescence as a phase in building one's connection to the values, beliefs, and practices of its religious and/or ethnic group. Given the disruption during adolescence that the revolution created, it is easy to see how this played a significant role in understanding the exile's sense of their Cuban Jewish identity. These narratives about identity have then been passed along to family members. Further, I asked all interviewees their thoughts on the importance of family and community to the Jewbans, both during their time in Cuba as well as in the US and in the three different generations. Universally there was agreement that family is the most important thing, even when there are significant disagreements. They believe this to be a Jewish thing and a value that was emphasized in Cuba as well, but not specifically a Jewban characteristic. Interrelated to family is community, as both in Cuba and in the US

Shiksa Speaks: A White, Non-Jew's Understanding of the
Cuban Jewish Diaspora and Its Legacy, 51–67.
Copyright © 2025 *Laura Finley*
Published under exclusive licence by Emerald Publishing Limited
HB: 978-1-83708-494-4, PB: 978-1-83708-495-1, ePDF: 978-1-83708-496-8

the family formed its own community with others, typically other Jewbans, added but never replacing family as the most important people.

EXILES AND IDENTITY

Consistent with Eckstein (2009), I found that the exiles I interviewed were very proud to identify their Cuban origins. This is true of Cubans in general, according to Eckstein (2009). "Cubans share a common language and common colonial cultural heritage with other Latin Americans. However, they tend to see themselves as different, and their experiences both in their homeland and their new land have been, in important respects, distinctive" (Eckstein, 2009, p. 2). As discussed in Chapter 7, they discuss Cuba as a paradise that welcomed their families and as a wonderful place to grow up before the revolution. They have passed this pride along to their children and their grandchildren. All who I interviewed, despite most never going to Cuba nor really knowing much about it, found it to be a point of pride that their grandparents took the enormous gamble leaving virtually everything at young ages to come to a new land. Yet none said that being Cuban was the most important part of their identity. Nor did they say being US citizens, which all are, was a key part of their identity, either. This is unlike Eckstein's (2009) research, in which she found that of the exiles, most identified as Cuban or Cuban-American. Only five percent of exiles identified as American. Powell (2022) explained that "as a group who lived through events that others can barely comprehend, they remember. Because for them memory is the foundation of identity" (p. 256).

Being Jewban was also mentioned with pride by all of the interviewees. It is the unique experience of the double diaspora that was echoed by everyone. Again, Eckstein (2009) found similarly when she noted that despite any overt discrimination or marginalization, Jews fleeing Cuba identified as refugees and the American government treated them as such. As Chapter 8 shows, the term refugee did not actually apply to Cubans at the time, at least not in the way the US government defined it. But, nonetheless, that narrative became part of the family's identity. The family narrative is one of the tragic loss of a beautiful home and businesses, a story of victimization by a horrible government. By comparison, it seems that any concerns expressed about politics today are met with a quick retort that we should feel blessed not to have to leave everything. For example, David and I have expressed deep concerns about the Trump presidency and the leadership of Florida Governor Ron DeSantis. We occasionally discuss the possibility of moving out of the state if not out of the country. Lilia always hushes us, reminding us that we've got it good in comparison to what she experienced.

Every one of the interviewees emphasized that their Jewishness is the most important part of their identity. This is likely due to the fact that Jewish culture and traditions were unwavering regardless of whether the family was in a new country. Perry expressed the following sentiment about his Jewishness: "I think my Jewish heritage is kinda part of my DNA of who I am and who I identify as.

Although not very religious, its history and traditions and teachings I think have led me to being a "good" person and have tried to live by. To be being [AQ: Is this correct?] Jewish, yes it's the traditions and stuff but more importantly its being a good kind thought full person and giving what you can when you can to your family and community." Rachel B. definitely identifies as Jewish but mostly commemorates the holidays, she does not regularly go to services but plans to raise her children Jewish. She said that Jewish education was very important to the family, but for the kids it was more about social programs. As a result of the importance of their Jewishness as well as the fact that no family remained in Cuba after 1962, this family is far more interested in and concerned about Israel than it is Cuba, outside of Ester. In fact, some reports suggest that many Jews had a chilled relationship with the Castro government not because it discriminated against them but rather because of the island's pro-Palestine opinion (Kaplan, 2001). Ester concurs that her family's grief at leaving the island "led them to disavow Cuba reaffirm our commitments to Jewish family continuity and material success" (Shapiro, 2018, pp. 160–161).

More on this commitment to Israel later in the chapter.

ON BEING JEWBAN

In cities like Miami, where many exiles lived, they set up grocery stores, shops, restaurants, and other small businesses and "created a milieu where island-born mingled, shopped, ate, drank, and 'talked Cuba'. Calle Ocho, Southwest Eighth Street, and Bergenline Avenue because the hubs of Little Havana and Union City (New Jersey), respectively. The areas maintained their Cuban flair and ethnic import, exile-defined, even after they were no longer majority Cuban and after the Cuba-born became enmeshed in broader city life" (Eckstein, 2009, p. 54). Most exiles celebrated Cuban holidays, for instance, the anniversary of Jose Marti's birth, and May 20, the day of Cuban independence. They also established museums and monuments. In Miami, veterans of the 1961 Bay of Pigs invasion established a museum. Downtown Miami is host to the Freedom Torch, which burns in commemoration of those who lost their lives trying to flee Castro. After the Elian Gonzalez debacle, the Cuban American National Foundation, dominated by exiles, transformed the home with whom Elian had stayed unto a museum. Parks and roads also bear the names of Cubans, for instance, Mazimo Gomez Park and Jorge Mas Canosa Blvd. There's also a middle school bearing Mas Canosa's name. Famed "Queen of Salsa" Celia Cruz has a road in tribute as well as a monument (Eckstein, 2009). Miami, then is filled with Cubanness and also Jewbanness. Similar, others with similar family histories identify more as Cuban Jews. Jewban Gigi Anders (2005) explained that "In Miami, Cubans know who they are. They never have to feel ashamed to be it. That's one of the things I love the most about going there, that instant unspoken understanding that *nosotros somos Cubanos* [We are Cubans]" (p. 138). Living in the Northeast, she wrote that she feels "very Cuban most of the time, especially in contrast to my New Yorker fiancé and his

North American family and most of the rest of the native English speakers in my northeastern life. I will nevertheless never feel as fanatically or defiantly Cuban, or as Cuban to the exclusion of all other things, as do my friends and family who left Cuba in the early sixties, moved to Miami, and haven't budged since" (p. 138).

Interestingly, this family celebrated their Jewbanness only minimally. For example, Gregg explained how he recalls the Cuban-Jewish identity growing up. This included Bar mitzvahs with Spanish music. Bobe and Zeide were pronounced differently than the American Jewish version, Bubbee and Zaydee. He also said he believes that Latin Jews in general are much louder and "more passionate" than American Jews, which he argued could be a good or a bad thing. The Cuban influence on their family was more in food, music, and learning Spanish. Growing up, he recalls watching "¿Que Pasa, USA?", the first bilingual sitcom. It follows the Cuban Pena family as they adjust to life in 1970s Miami. Lisette expressed similar experiences. She tells people she is Jewban, but mostly the Cuban influence is in holidays with mixed traditions, where foods like Jewish brisket are served with Cuban beans and rice and plantains. She said she passed along the Jewbanness to her kids in that Spanish was their first language. Gregg's brother Jeff said that his Dad's side did not really emphasize Jewishness; in fact, he believes that his dad might have disavowed religion were it not for family and social pressure. He was more into Cuban culture, especially food and music. He had a Cuban instrument and had some Cuban friends, even non-Jews. As kids they hated it because he blared Cuban music loudly in the car and they were embarrassed but now he appreciates Latin music, not just Cuban, though. They spoke Spanish at home, but he is no longer fluent as he does not live in South Florida so rarely uses it. Perry responded that his Cuban heritage is more an honor to my mom and dad. He wrote in a personal correspondence, "I don't have any feeling or link to the land per se, but I do to Cuban music and food and struggle. Some interesting things to note would be that people get quite surprised when I start speaking fluent Spanish with a name like Bekerman....both non-Jewish Cubans and Americans as well. That's when of course you need to explain the history. I also wonder too does being born in a place automatically make you a "ban or can" of that country. I guess it does, but it goes back to the questions are you more "Jew" or more "ban"...or could we be Cubish....LMAO." He says that one of his biggest regrets is not having properly taught my kids Spanish although they understand fairly well and speak it conversationally. Jodi, Perry's wife, has known him since she was 12. Her father was a Youth Director where they both hung out. Until then, she did not know "Jewbans" were a thing. Her dad later moved to work with the Miami Beach synagogue where there were a lot of Jewbans. Jodi said that her family does not really identify as Jewban, more as Jews that speak Spanish and like Cuban food and music.

This same connection to Jewbanness was passed along to Lilia's grandchildren. Rachel B., granddaughter of Jack and Lilia and daughter of David, explained her relationship to Jewbanness. Likes considering herself Jewban, it "makes me special." She is not as immersed in it, though, given her parent's divorce when she was an infant and them living separately. She acknowledged that family get togethers, especially the food, had a more Cuban flavor than did those of her American Jewish friends. Even the brisket is made differently. Rachel said she tried learning Spanish but is not fluent, although like Perry's kids she can understand and get by if needed. Similarly, Dylan, grandson of Lilia and Jack, explained that he only partly identifies as Cuban. He said that thinks of Cuba as the family's most recent journey, not as a deep part of who they are. He does not recall much in terms of Cubanness in their immediate family, stating that they did not visit sites or festivals, for instance. Like the others, he said that food at family gatherings and the learning of Spanish were pretty much it. Yet still, Dylan said he is proud to be a Jewish Cuban. He did note that it is hard outside of Miami and certain other cities, though, as people don't really understand what a Jewban is. He found this while studying in Madison, Wisconsin and in Boulder, Colorado, so took to omitting the Cuban part and simply explaining to others that he is Jewish. Granddaughter Ashley, the oldest, explained that as a child she was uncertain of how Cuban she was. She enjoys the food and coffee but didn't see anyone outside of her grandparents as really being Cuban. She believed that they were not supposed to speak Spanish at home because her grandparents went through so much to get here from Cuba, and they wanted everyone to be "American." In reality, Lilia and Jack were unhappy that they did not get taught much Spanish at home! Also, Ashley does not look "Latin," while her sister Stephanie does, so no one ever mistook her for Cuban. In college she was able to "check the Latino box," which brought some advantages, and she got more into understanding her Latin heritage, joining clubs, and learning Latin dance. Her husband Scott reminded her that not one in her family is really Cuban except her grandparents who were born there, so she sometimes feels like an imposter. She does not really know a lot about her family's time in Cuba but always thought of it as beautiful until it got scary and uncertain. Stephanie explained that a challenge she has faced is that, of all in the family, she is the one who looks most "Latin" and least "Jewish." She speaks and understands some Spanish, but people often presume she knows more. People have asked how being Cuban and Jewish can even "be a thing." She is asked often where she is from and people don't want to accept when she says, "South Florida." Like the others, the influence of Cuban culture was mostly food and music. Her mom grew up kosher, so they had no pork, with the exception of ham croquetas—a Cuban specialty. She wishes her parents has taught her more Spanish and recalls her grandparents telling them that they should. She is currently studying Spanish on Duolingo so that she can brush up. Stephanie noted that despite growing up in South Florida, she does not recall learning much about Cuba at school or at home. She knows the basics about her grandparents leaving when they got married and that Castro seized their businesses but does not really recall anyone telling specific stories about their time in Cuba.

Allan, Ashley and Stephanie's brother, was the one of that generation who identifies most as Jewban. He said he did not always think about it but getting older he realizes how their holidays and traditions were a blend of Jewishness and Cuban. Further, he works in the baseball industry so is more interested in Cuba's rich baseball tradition. Similarly, he loves to cook so has explored making Cuban dishes, including for several years Cuban Lechon Asado, a roast pig, on New Years Eve. To Ashley's point, all the children and grandchildren identified as Hispanic for advantages when applying to college.

David is definitely the most connected to the family's Jewban heritage. He is both proud of it and interested in learning about the family tree, their experiences in Cuba, and their travels and reception in the US. He is the most social of his siblings and spent a lot of time when he was young with both grandmothers and with his maternal grandfather, so knows more of their stories than even his mom does. He also knows more about all of the extended family than anyone in the family.

ON JEWISHNESS

This family emphasized their Jewishness, although none routinely attend services at a synagogue. Lilia has, since the coronavirus pandemic, attended virtual services every Friday and all attend a virtual service for certain holidays. All do fast for the Yom Kippur, though, which makes the more devout than the average Jew in America, as research shows that less than half fast for all or part of it. Pew Research shows that they are not the norm in emphasizing their Jewishness, as Jews are much less likely than Christians (28% to 57%) to say that religion is very important in their lives. The report noted that, "among Jews as a whole, far more report that they find meaning in spending time with their families or friends, engaging with arts and literature, being outdoors, and pursuing their education or careers than find meaning in their religious faith. Twice as many Jewish Americans say they derive a great deal of meaning and fulfillment from spending time with pets as say the same about their religion. And yet, even for many Jews who are not particularly religious, Jewish identity matters: Fully three-quarters of Jewish Americans say that "being Jewish" is either very important (42%) or somewhat important (34%) to them" (Pew Research Center, 2021).Jeff and his wife Becky, who is Jewish but not Jewban, pass Jewishness on to their kids but not really their Cuban heritage. Difficult because they moved away, and the kids don't live in a place like Miami where it resonates. Likewise, Lisette and Perry both noted the importance of passing along their Jewishness and raising their children in the Jewish tradition. Ashley and Stephanie both noted that their Judaism is unwavering. Consistent with the Pew Research Center (2021) findings, however, this family did emphasize the cultural components of Judaism. "Many American Jews prioritize cultural components of Judaism over religious ones. Most Jewish adults say that remembering the Holocaust, leading a moral and ethical life, working for justice and equality in society, and being intellectually curious are "essential" to what it means to them to be Jewish."

Although it did not come up in all of the interviews, David and his immediate family (Rachel B., Lilia, Lisette and her family, and Perry and his family) all have repeatedly expressed a deep love for Israel. Apparently, Isaac Schigiel was a Zionist and at one point hosted Menachem Began in their home in Cuba. This is consistent with research, as the Pew Research Center (2021) found that eight in ten American Jews said Israel is an important part of what being Jewish means to them. Everyone in the family has been to Israel, most multiple times. All of the kids studied in Israel and all but Ethan, the youngest grandson went on Birthright (he missed it because it was cancelled due to the coronavirus pandemic). Everyone went to Hebrew school. As I write the war between Israel and the militant group Hamas continues to rage on, which has led to some heated discussions in our home. In brief, Hamas militants staged a horrific surprise assault on Israel on October 7, 2023, infiltrating the country by air, land, and sea. More than 1,200 Israelis were killed and 240 people were taken as hostages. Israel responded by waging full on war, with the support of the US, its biggest ally and contributor of military aid and weapons. As of January 13, 2025, the death toll has topped 46,000 and Gaza, the portion of the land in which most Palestinians reside, has been reduced to rubble. I have long been involved in peace activism and have a difficult time with the blind support for Israel and its continued attacks on civilians. Yet polls show most American Jews support the war, despite its extensive toll on innocent civilians and approve of President Biden's continued aid to Israel, This is despite members of his own administration and the United Nations calling for more pressure on Israel to stop its onslaught (Gans & Manchester, 2024).

Ester is the only one who overtly expressed any sentiment that was not glowing about Israel, although she did it in writing, not in our interview (the topic did not come up). She wrote "I traveled to Israel only once, in 1990, visiting my Abuela Berta's youngest sister, my great-aunt, Yochebed and the family she established in Palestine in 1936 when she took charge of her ailing mother who refused to immigrate to pagan Cuba. I found the open expressions of racism towards Arab and Palestinian communities and justification of violently imposed occupation intolerable, and I have been unable to return" (Shapiro, 2018, p. 167).

ON FAMILY

In their study of Cuban Jews still living on the island, LaPorte et al. (2009) shed some light on family values that are both Cuban and Jewish. They assert that generally Cuban families are similar to those in other Latin American family, characterized by loyalty and unity. Generations often live together or nearby. They also found that the Cuban Jewish community takes care of other Jews and pass along to their families an "ethic of caring."

Half of the Jewish population of the world lived in the shtetls of Eastern Europe in the 19th century. Portrayed as harsh, for example in "Fiddler on the Roof," shtetl life was also focused on family, community, and commitment (Hant, 2011).

Rok (Ester) wrote about their family connectedness that started in Eastern Europe. She wrote,

> In telling the story of my Cuban Easter European Jewish self, I listen closely to a competing cacophony of ancestral voices carrying 150 years of oral history and living memory, because among them I discern the currents of my own life. I must reconstruct the disconnected narrative of a family life unfolding in a turn-of-the-century Russian-Polish border shtetl village and then transplanted across three continents, two world wars, two revolutions, and five languages" (p. 230). Her father was deeply attached to his parents Berta and Lazaro and to his brother Noel. She described how the family formed "intense ties of mutual protection and loyalty in the long passage from the shtetl in Rubyshevish, Belarus to the rural Cuban village of Bolondron. (p. 230)

In another piece, Ester reflected on her family

> Looking back in intergenerational time and space for this narrative, I see how I was fortunate to grow up in my close-knit, polyglot, Polish/Byelorussian Jewish extended family in Havana, later transplanted to South Florida, lovingly cherished by my two intrepid, determined, though domineering grandmothers, who survived wars and revolutions across continents encompassing most of the 20th century and the dawn of the 21st. Their living examples spoke more enduringly to me than their silent collusion in often violent family enforcement of strict patriarchal roles and materialistic values, particularly those restricting my educational aspirations, viewed as encouraging my disobedience and endangering my marriage prospects and future as a wife and mother, prohibitions I fiercely fought. (Shapiro, 2018, p. 170)

All the family lived near one another in Havana. As people married, the extended family grew. While their journeys from Cuba to the US stretched over nearly two years, eventually all of the extended family again lived near one another in South Florida. When they lived in New York, Lilia and Jack lived in the same housing complex as did Consuelo and Isaac and Eva. Family did not always get along but did things together regardless. They still do. Some also spend significant time not talking with family members—a concept with which I was no familiar unless there is some serious issue like abuse. The same is true of these families when they came to the US, they tended to stay close, at least physically. While at first people were a bit spread out, in short time most everyone lived in South Florida. Today, some of the extended family has moved away but my husband's immediate family all live within 15 minutes of one another. They are mishpachah. Greenspoon (2016) explained "Dictionary definitions of the term mishpachah are quite similar: a Jewish family or social unit including close and distant relatives—sometimes also close friends. Although such definitions—or better, descriptions—are justifiably inclusive, even they fail to capture the diversity and vitality of real flesh-and-blood Jewish families" (p. ix).

Family has also been instrumental in the financial successes of this family and of the Jewbans in general. Those who have done well have given loans to others who wish to start businesses. None of the second or third generation had to pay for higher education, as their family's took care of it. This is obviously a huge advantage in the US, where college costs are exorbitant, and many young people graduate with serious debt. Further, family has provided employment opportunities. David runs the family jewelry business, which is 50 years old and had its precursor in Cuba. Ester expressed that there were always family tensions around money. Her mother was the favorite of grandmother Berta because she was shy and meek but also because she was wealthy. At the time she married in 1951 her dowry was $10,000, equivalent to approximately $125,000 today. It is with this that her father and the Shapiros started the hardware business in Cuba. The family does not like to think about or discuss Cuban privileges in the US.

Ester discussed the closeness of her family and the South Floridan Jewban community, albeit in not entirely glowing terms. "Required to speak Spanish at home and to socialize exclusively within our extended family, we were forbidden to have non-Jewish friends, locating our Cuban identities narrowly within politically conservative Miami Cuban Jewish communities" (Shapiro, 2018, p. 161). She also reflected, "I look back on our often courageous, at times meanly competitive, and always forward-looking family with admiration and compassion. with righteous anger when necessary to my survival, and with determination to live by my values" (Shapiro, 2018, p. 173).

Women hold a special place in Jewban families it seems. Cuban families tend to be matrifocal, with the mother at the head of the household (Safa, 2009). This is definitely true of my husband's grandparents and his parents, and to a lesser degree to the subsequent generations. The matrifocal arrangement may also be connected to the Jewishness. Jewish mothers are stereotyped as meddlesome and hovering yet loveable and respected. The older generations were quite patriarchal, but the women were strong and, in many ways, led the family. Ester described her grandmothers:

> Mis abuelas [my grandmothers] differed in many ways—my maternal Abuela Adela. the youngest in her family, arrived in Cuba as an adventurous, sociable adolescent and responded open-heartedly to the openness of a multiracial Cuban culture, in ways exemplified by her exuberant Cuban Jewish cooking and hospitable open-door policy. Introduced to her husband. my reticent Abuelo Salomon, through an island-wide network identifying eligible Jewish bachelors, she spoke to us in a mix of accented Spanish with some Yiddish, reflecting her Cuban transculturation. My paternal grandmother. Abuela Berta, became the responsible oldest and co-parent after the accidental deaths of her father and oldest brother coincided with the start of World War 1. She fell in love with my handsome, pampered, frail Abuelo Lazaro and formed her young family on the Russian Polish border. This included her eldest, my exuberant Aunt Consuela, lovingly remembered; her middle son. my taciturn Uncle Noel; and my father, Jaime. her youngest and favorite child—their lives always on the edge of famine or catastrophe until their just-in-time immigration to rural Cuba in 1936. Abuela Berta was far more guarded with outsiders: speaking to us in Yiddish mixed with Polish and Russian, she sternly warned that friends could always

betray and only family could be trusted. Her desiccated, Polish-style holiday brisket was untouched by Cuban influences, food consumed for survival only; her bereaved family survived during World War I when their home was seized for a military hospital thanks to her mother's ingenious recipe for potato peel soup made from commissary discards (Shapiro, 2018, p. 171).

Ester also described how Aunt Consuelo was treated. "To hear Abuela Berta tell our family stories, her daughter, my exuberant Tia Consuelo, was a source of eternal danger requiring constant maternal vigilance until she was finally married off and became her husband's concern" (Rok, 1999, p. 231). She went on,

> Consuelo's voluptuous body, her exuberant personality, and her blond-haired, green-eyed exotic beauty initiated a flurry of unacceptable courtships from important men in Bolondron. My grandparents charged her two younger brothers with her surveillance so my grandfather could deliver beatings, though these did not succeed in stopping her unacceptable non-Jewish romances. By the time Consuelo was 17, she was twice married through arrangements in the Havana Jewish community" (Shapiro, 2018, p. 168).

Ester, like her Aunt Consuelo, was outspoken and sexual and this was not acceptable at the time and especially by this family. A woman's value was in what her body could bring to the highest bidder in terms of who they married, and so many marriages were arranged among the Cuban Jews expressly for that purpose. Her sister Rachel added that family was always very critical and quick to share their criticism of you and gossip/backstab. But they still got together because you were obligated to be present. Many people cut others out of their lives, at least for stretches of time, like Lilia and Leo and Sam Shapiro and Leo. Leo only came to see him when Sam was dying. She described Leo as being difficult, like their dad. Lilia was nice, with a big personality like her mother. Ester was the first to move to Boston for grad school and then she followed. Her dad would not speak to her for a long time, and their parents did not even go to Ester's wedding to Alan because they were upset he was not Jewish. They did not like her first husband either because he had previously been married. Rachel said she believes that intergenerational trauma led to family distrust. She also recalls lots of arranged marriages between Jews, usually within the same type, as the Ashkenazi family, especially in Eastern Europe and Cuba, frowned on intermarriage with the Sephardic. Helen said Jews were not supposed to marry non-Jews even in the US, and that Eva actually wanted Enrique to marry a Cuban Jew.

This is no longer an issue, at least among the family members I am closest to. Lisette's husband Alan in part Sephardic (his parents did have an intermarriage in Cuba before moving here). I am not Jewish, although two of David's previous wives were and the third converted. Rachel B.'s husband Derek is not Jewish either. Gregg also expressed that there was always a lot of drama in the family. He mentioned this issue with Isaac's sister Ryfka. She was the first to immigrate to Cuba and he had difficulty getting out of Poland. Everyone else died in the camps but she "saved" him, so he always felt beholden to her. This made his relationship with Consuelo strained, as he spent a lot of time with his sister, disregarding in part his own wife and family.

Ester wrote about the role of women in Cuba:

> First in Cuba, then later in Cuban Jewish enclaves in South Florida, both abuelas honored rules and roles of Cuban Jewish patriarchy while, at the same time, clearly subverting them: they ran successful family businesses through multiple migrations, while elevating their husbands and sons into positions of business and family authority and marrying off their daughters as required by tradition. Both adored me as a bookish, observant, and curious girl, entrusting me with cherished family stories of struggle and survival. Yet they also unquestioningly accepted my father's often violent enforcement of his patriarchal authority over his wife and three daughters. As in many other periods of history. women may be called on to take the men's role during times of crisis, but patriarchy like all forms of power protects its privileges, and societies return to traditional gender roles for continuity and security. In our family, traditional gender roles became even more entrenched as our transplanted multigenerational family achieved economic success. (Shapiro, 2018, p. 171)

As Bolen (1985), wrote,

> "...no more important figure has been depicted than the shtetl yiddisheh mammeh (Jewish mother), the stalwart foundation of the family, without whom the family could not survive. This is the mother figure that represents maternal instinct by "providing physical, psychological or spiritual nourishment to others" (p. 172). The Jewish shtetl mothers stands by her family no matter what. Zborowski (1962) explained that Jewish mothers express their love for their children in two primary ways: "by unremitting solicitude about every aspect of her child's welfare, expressed for the most part in unceasing verbalization" and "by constant and solicitous overfeeding." (p. 293)

Jewish mothers in the shtetl developed the practice of offering their children an excessive amount of food, a symbol of their love, and the rejection of food can be viewed as a rejection of that love. Zborwoski and Herzog (1962) explained "A child soon learns that he can coerce his seniors into yielding on almost any point by refusing to eat...the rejection of food means rejection of loved ones and life itself. It is intolerable and excites acute anxiety" (p. 303). Jewish mothers constantly remind their children of all the sacrifices they have made for them and are always worried for their children. "Worry is not viewed as an indulgence but as an expression of affection and almost a duty. If you worry actively enough, something may come of it" (Zborowski & Herzog, 1962, p. 294). From the shtetl also came a number of superstitions. For instance, babies are not to be praised too much because the "evil eye" may be encouraged to cause havoc with the child (In Hant, 2011). David has occasionally called his mother yiddishe mammeh and sang the song with that title. Lilia is definitely a classic pusher of food and a worrier, but as Zborwoski and Herzog (1962) explained, it is clear that it is an expression of love. She has passed these qualities on to her children, although more than the others, to David. For example, when we travel, the first thing David does, as soon as cell service is available, is text his mom to tell her we landed, even when we have traveled internationally and the time zones are way different. He, Perry, and Lisette sometimes refrain from telling Lilia about minor aches and pains or about other things that may worry her. He is also a worrier and food pusher! For example, if I go for a walk to the store, all of 1 ½ miles round trip, he always reminds me to let him know when I get safely there and safely home. It makes me smile, as it is hard to see how my short walk to the local Publix is a high-danger situation.

The mothers in this family also seem to have a special place in their hearts for their sons. This may be a Jewish quality, a Jewban one, or just a family characteristic. Ester has written about her grandmother Berta's immense love for her sons and her difficulties with her daughter Consuelo. Anders discussed the male privilege as well, expressing that she had to "confront the profound Hispanic reality and dirty not-so-little secret that no matter how much your parents love you, they will always prefer their sons. You have eggs. Your brothers have penises. It's as simple as that. It's a general worldview, boys and girls are not equally valued" (p. 121). As a non-Jew, it is interesting to observe the mother-son relationship. It is very strong, perhaps even intimate, although that word has connotations I do not intend. But as I see it, the closeness as an outsider to the family and to Judaism feels a bit much at times. Sometimes even like, as a wife, I am lower priority. David and his mother, who lives only 15 minutes away and still works in the office of their mail order business at least once per week, talk on the phone at minimum twice per day. He has answered the phone when she calls during the middle of dinner, even if he already spoke to her that day. I have learned that this may be a Jewish thing between mothers and sons, but not one that is rooted in Jewish doctrine. In Judaism, a couple walks through the chuppah, a wedding canopy, with their parents during their wedding. Once that is done, the bride and groom are to leave their parents behind and walk toward a new life together.

The Jewish American Princess (JAP) is another stereotype that has, in my research, some applicability to this family, albeit in a good way. Although the term often refers to a young woman who is spoiled, I see that the women in this family are assertive and get what they want because they ask for it. Rachel B., for example, is always polite and respectful but is not shy to ask for refunds for services she finds dissatisfying, something I find to be very difficult. Lilia is well-known in the family for returning items to stores that she believes are not up to par, even things like avocados she thinks are too ripe. Yet both do this with wonderful smiles and pleasant demeanors. Anders described a version of the JAP unique to those of Cuban descent, the Jubana. In her book *Jubana! The awkwardly true and dazzling adventures of a Jewish Cubana goddess*, Gigi Anders tells stories similar to those I have heard and experienced with my husband's family. Her parents were exiles who fled Castro as well and who continue to refer to him as the devil. Her mother's focus in life is to prepare her daughter to get married, which she begins when Gigi is an infant. Her mother is a domineering and controlling figure, but Gigi loves and admires her, wanting to be like her. In her family, appearances are very important. The women do not go out without makeup, they spend money on getting their hair and nails done and on nice clothes. And, on therapy. They are not shy to seek assistance from any type of medical professional. Anders also discussed that many members of the family, herself included, deal with depression. She questions whether it could be a "chemical of genetic hand-me-down," derived from the traumas of the Holocaust death camps and passed down the generations. Lilia describes her mother as always immaculately made up, and she too is always well-dressed and still gets her hair dyed and her nails done at 80 years old. Ester wrote about how Consuelo made fun of her African beads once, asking when her husband would buy her "real" jewelry. The family not only knows a doctor for virtually every specialty, but routinely seeks second and even third opinions on medical issues.

One thing I have noticed about this family is the propensity to interrupt or speak over people. I am still adjusting to this and trying (not always successfully, I admit) not to get upset when it feels like I cannot get a complete sentence into a conversation. I am told this is because they are "passionate," but to me that seems like an excuse. I and many others are "passionate" about lots of topics but still wait our turn to speak. Deborah Tannen has studied this and calls it collaborative overlapping. She explained "cooperative overlapping occurs when the listener starts talking along with the speaker, not to cut them off but rather to validate or show they're engaged in what the other person is saying." It is unclear whether this is a Cuban thing, a Jewban thing, or neither, but I suspect it is related to their identity at least in part. Tannen found that it was especially common in Jewish people from the Northeast. This family spent years there (Borresen, 2021).

The "passion" also sometimes seems to me aggression. This is especially true when driving is involved! I have not ridden in a vehicle driven by all of my interviewees so cannot say that they all do it, but those who I have ridden drive very aggressively and are easily angered by other drivers—sometimes appropriately, as they do dumb things, but sometimes for the very things they are themselves doing! Of course, this is also partly a South Florida issue, as driving here is notoriously treacherous. And I know that as a Michigan "friendly" driver as well as one who had a terrible accident a few years ago (getting t-boned by a driver going the wrong way on a one-way street), I may be more sensitive to this.

There is also, it seems, a tendency to want to tell people what to do, and to get upset if they choose to do otherwise. Again, that could be unrelated to Cubanness/ Jewishness/Jewbanness, but I suspect it is related at least in some way. For example, David loves to tell me where I need to park when we arrive at a destination, as if I cannot figure it out! In riding with Lilia, I learned she is the same.

ON COMMUNITY

As noted in Chapter 2, many Cuban Jews reported to Bettinger-López (2000) that the Jewish community in Miami was not very welcoming to them when they arrived by the thousands in 1959 and the early 1960s. Reportedly they provided no financial aid or moral support. Some have said that even the Greater Miami Jewish Federation did not immediately offer assistance, so Cuban Jews had to establish their own synagogues and groups. Also, American Jews were aware of federal support being offered so did not feel it necessary to add to that. Garcia (1996) explained that many of Miami's poor, working class people resented the Cuban migrants for the various supports they received. Cuban Jews who emigrated to other parts of the country, especially New York, reported better experiences. Yet others paint a rosier picture of the reception of Jewbans in Miami. Levine (2010) reported that the Greater Miami Jewish Federation (GMJF) set up a reception center at the airport and were joined by other welfare agencies. Help was also provided by the Hebrew Immigrant Aid Society (HIAS) as well as the National Council of Jewish Women (NCJW). Kahn (1981) reported that even the exiles who did not have connections to Miami previously were able to redeem Israel Bonds that had been purchased in Cuba, such that only 808 resettled Jews required extensive assistance from Jewish organizations, although Bettinger-López corrected that this figure was only based on help provided by HIAS, not other aid organizations. Local media outlets expressed the position that the Cuban influx was a burden and a drain on resources. In contrast, national media as well as government and religious leaders treated the Cuban migrants as heroic refugees (Bettinger-López, 2000).

In Miami, the only established congregation that sought to welcome the Ashkenazi from Cuba was the Conservative Temple Menorah on Miami Beach. But, by 1966, most Cuban Jews were accepted as part of the Greater Miami Jewish community and in particular to the Greater Miami Jewish Federation, which they said had rejected them six years prior (Bettinger-López, 2000). In Miami Beach, the Cuban-Hebrew Congregation of Miami—Beth Kneseth Szmuel Szechter became a hub of Cuban Jewish life and remained that way for decades. The latter half is called Temple Beth Schmuel, but others recall its earlier version and refer to it as El Circulo. It was not just a location for religious services but also a place for socialization, a characteristic of Cuban Jews. It was modeled after the Patronato in Havana. Just as in Havana, women played an active role in developing it (Bettinger-López, 2000).

In contrast to the Jewbans I interviewed, LaPorte et al. (2009) found that Cuban Jews on the island felt that their Judaism had been influenced by the collectivist nature of Cuba. Rather than the large family affairs the Bekerman family holds, Jewish holidays are spent with others at the synagogue. One person they interviewed even expressed, "In the rest of the world Jews support their synagogue; in Cuba, the synagogue supports the Jews."

In South Florida, Cuban exiles and their families have long been critical in shaping local politics. Over the more than 60 years that some have been here, they have come to influence state and national politics as well. Over time, the exile Cuban Americans became a powerful voting block, owing in large part to the advantage they had to become citizens. By 1980, 60 percent of Cubans across the nation and 51 percent living in Miami were citizens with 56 and 47 percent, respectively, of voting age. They took candidates' stance on Cuba into consideration when voting, supporting candidates that were opposed to Castro or anything they associated with socialism. The Cuban American community elected their own to local, state and eventually national positions. In 1989, Ileana Ros-Lehtinen was the first Cuban immigrant elected to Congress, followed by Lincoln Diaz-Balart and Robert Menendez (Eckstein, 2022). In 2000, Cuban exiles and other Cuban immigrants cast important votes in the close presidential election that was declared a win for George W. Bush. As Girard et al. (2012) wrote, "The literature suggests that the partisan allegiance of Cuban Americans is fueled by fierce opposition to the Castro regime in Cuba. Indeed, for over one-half century, the anti-Castro views of most migrants from Cuba have been woven into an 'exile' ideology. This world view is woven into a strong sense among Cuban Americans of having lost their homeland" (p. 43). Further, the Bay of Pigs fiasco cemented distrust of Democrats, as did 1972 Democrat presidential candidate George McGovern's promise to normalize relations with Cuba (Girard et al., 2012). This family, however, has not been very active politically, outside of voting in general elections. The exiles have generally voted Republican, but the younger generations lean more Democrat. Lilia has expressed that she did not like President Obama, in large part due to efforts he made to open up relations with Cuba.

The Cuban-Jewish community tends to view more recent Cuban emigres as different and does not engage much. "Since a part of the hard-line anti-Castro position entails labeling Cubans who have remained in revolutionary Cuba as Communists, Castro-lovers, and traitors to the 'real' Cuba—the Cuba of the past—the Cuban-Jewish community views these recent Jewish-Cuban emigres with ambivalence. On the one hand, it is believed, these are fellow Jews and thus should be welcomed into the community. On the other hand, however, these people often are assumed to be Communists-perhaps even infiltrators for the Castro government—and thus may not 'belong' in a community which, as explicitly states in its list of general provisions and objectives, is democratic in spirit and wholly allied with the United States against Fidel Castro" (Bettinger-López, 2000, pp. xl-xli).

As Eckstein (2022) writes, there was (and remains) a fairly sharp divide between the self-defined exiles of the 1960s and 1970s and the "New Cubans" who came in subsequent decades. "The divide, in part, was class-based. According to a 2014 Miami survey by Florida International University, among the earlier emigres 6 percent viewed themselves as upper class, 75 percent as middle or upper middle class, and 18 percent as lower middle class. In contrast, among those who emigrated after 1995 only 1 percent considered themselves upper class; 45 percent considered themselves middle or upper middle class, and 32 percent considered themselves lower middle class. About twenty times more of the recent than the earlier emigres considered themselves lower class. Poor new Cubans were likely to draw on welfare, which became politicized" (p. 261). This wealth gap is reflected in the jobs held by the earlier versus newer emigres. Twice as many of the earlier Cuban migrants held high-status jobs and three times as many were in the top tercile of US income earners. While these differences reflect the different demographics of who emigrated from Cuba, they are reflect the extremely generous benefits afforded through the Cuban Refugee Program. Another part of the divide was in their attitude toward the island. The earlier exiles opposed any ties to Cuba, with most never returning nor even staying very aware of what was happening in their home country. The New Cubans wanted to remain tied to the island, as many still had family there while the earlier exiles did not (Eckstein, 2022). Although he did not express these concerns about Cubans who immigrated in more recent years, Dylan said he does not feel connected to the Cuban community in Miami. In part he said that he recognizes that his family is whiter than many Cubans in Miami today and more affluent.

The "community" for this family, especially Lilia and her generation living in South Florida, is almost exclusively Jewban. Jeff expressed that the family belonged to a tight community in Cuba and many Jewbans recreated that in Miami. Jeff and Gregg's described how their mother in particular remained friends with other Jewban exiles, all who lived near them in North Miami. Lilia still gets together with Jewbans with whom she went to school in Cuba and who live in South Florida. This is less-so for the later generations, although outside of David, their friend circles tend to be largely Jewish, if not Jewban.

CONCLUSION

There are so many factors that shape our sense of identity. It has been interesting to learn more about Cubanness versus Jewishness and Jewbanness as well as how and why each influences the identity of my participants. Having admired the closeness of this family, it was fascinating to learn of the many rifts and dramas as well. I have also enjoyed learning more about the Jewban community in South Florida in general and can definitely see that part of the reason for its successes is family and community support. Not all immigrant groups have both in the ways that Jewbans do in South Florida.

REFERENCES

Anders, G. (2005). *Jubana! The awkwardly true and dazzling adventures of a Jewish Cubana goddess.* HarperCollins.

Bettinger-López, C. (2000). *Cuban-Jewish journeys: Searching for identity, home, and history in Miami.* University of Tennessee Press.

Bolen, J. (1985). *Goddesses in every woman: A new psychology of women.* Harper Perennial.

Borresen, K. (2021, March 4). How to know if you're an interrupter or a 'cooperative overlapper." *Huffington Post.* https://www.huffpost.com/entry/interrupting-or-coop-erative-overlapping_l_603e8ae9c5b601179ec0ff4e

Eckstein, S. (2009). *The immigrant divide: How Cuban Americans changed the U.S. and their homeland.* Routledge.

Eckstein, S. (2022). *Cuban privilege: The making of immigrant inequality in America.* Cambridge University Press.

Gans, J., & Manchester, J. (2024, January 3). Jewish American support for Biden stands firm amid Israel-Hamas war. *The Hill.* https://thehill.com/homenews/campaign/4385816-jewish-american-support-for-biden-stands-firm-amid-israel-hamas-war/

Garcia, M. (2009). *Havana USA: Cuban exiles and Cuban Americans in South Florida, 1959–1994.* University of California Press.

Girard, C., Grenier, G., & Gladwin, H. (2012). Exile politics and Republican party af-filiation: The case of Cuban Americans in Miami. *Social Science Quarterly, 93*(1), 42–57.

Greenspoon, J. (Ed.) (2016). *Mishpachah: The Jewish family in tradition and transition.* Purdue University Press.

Hant, M. (2011). A history of Jewish mothers on television: Decoding the tenacious stereo-type. *Journal of Interdisciplinary Feminist Thought, 5*(1), 1–23.

LaPorte, H., Sweifache, J., & Strug, D. (2009). Jewish life in Cuba today. *Journal of Jewish Communal Service, 84*(3/4), 313–324.

Levine, R. (2010). *Tropical diaspora: The Jewish experience in Cuba.* Markus Weiner Publisher.

Pew Research Center. (2021, May 11). *Jewish Americans in 2020.* https://www.pe-wresearch.org/religion/2021/05/11/economics-and-well-being-among-u-s-jews/#:~:text=As%20a%20whole%2C%20U.S.%20Jews,U.S.%20households%20at%20that%20level

Powell, D. (2022). *Ninety miles and a lifetime away: Memories of early Cuban exiles.* University Press of Florida.

Rok, E. (1999). From Belarus to Bolondron: A daughter's dangerous passage. In Agosin, M. (Ed.) *The house of memory: Stories by Jewish women writers of Latin America* (pp. 230–240). Feminist Press at the City University of New York.

Safa, H. (2009). Hierarchies and household change in postrevolutionary Cuba. *Latin American Perspectives, 36*(1), 42–52.

Shapiro, E. (2018). Transforming development through just communities: A lifelong jour-ney of inquiry. Latina Psychologists: *Thriving in the Borderland*, 158–175.

Zborowski, M., & Herzog, E. (1962). *Life is with people: The culture of the shtetl.* Schock-en Books.

CHAPTER 4

RISK-TAKING, WORK ETHIC, AND RESILIENCE

As noted in the Introduction, the Jewbans as a whole, and this family specifically, have been quite successful professionally and with it, financially. This success is consistent with what research shows about Jews in the US. A Pew Research poll in 2020 found that roughly half of Jews said their annual household income was at least $100,000, much higher than the percentage of US households overall at that level. More than 80 percent described their lives as satisfying, including their family life, physical health, and community (Pew Research Center, 2021). I was curious as to what factors might be responsible for this success. I also want to be careful not to reinforce any stereotypes of greedy or money-hungry Jews, as that is not my intent. Nor is it accurate in this case. Jack, for instance, is well-known for donating to any cause that sent him a request for money! In my interviews, the willingness to take risks and to work hard routinely came up. Further, most interviewees mentioned that Jews are resilient, having had to be as their families have been uprooted and faced centuries of discrimination. The narrative seems to be one of suffering and enduring, which allows little space to discuss advantages. What was not really mentioned was the immigration privileges afforded to the exile generation nor of the other types of assistance that helped their businesses

Shiksa Speaks: A White, Non-Jew's Understanding of the
Cuban Jewish Diaspora and Its Legacy, 69–79.
Copyright © 2025 *Laura Finley*
Published under exclusive licence by Emerald Publishing Limited
HB: 978-1-83708-494-4, PB: 978-1-83708-495-1, ePDF: 978-1-83708-496-8

be successful. I only learned about most of these through reviewing literature, from my discussion with Ester, and from subtle comments made by several interviewees or picked up over time around the family. The issues of privilege and advantages are addressed in more detail in Chapter 6.

ON SUCCESS

Burstein (2007) identified several factors that explain why Jews are more successful economically and educationally that are other racial, ethnic, and religious groups in the US. Educationally, by the 1950s American Jews exceeded the non-Jewish median level of education by 1.7 years, and by the 1970s that was up to 2.5 years. By the 1990s, more than 60 percent of Jews were college graduates. This is in comparison to 22 percent of non-Jews in the US. The occupational status of Jews has also been different than non-Jews, with Jews to hold professional positions. Owing to the pay of these positions Jews' household income is greater than other groups, as is their overall wealth. One reason proposed for this success is simple: devotion to education that results in higher paying jobs. This would then not be unique to Jews. Another theory emphasizes Jewish peculiarity. It proposes that Jewish education specifically encourages success in life, not in the afterlife, and emphasizes mutual assistance that benefits all. Third, perhaps it is Jews historical marginality that has forced them to be more innovative and to work harder through tough times. Finally, it may be owing to the closeness of Jewish communities that Jews are able to develop important social and human capital needed for success. Quantitative data best supports the latter explanation (Burstein, 2007). One of the exiles interviewed by Powell (2022) expressed why he felt they were successful in Miami, although he was not speaking specifically about Jewbans. "Take any country in the world—name it, I don't care—and take away people who are professional, and highly skilled labor, and decent people who do not agree with totalitarianism, and people who own business—put them together in a place, how do you expect their going to do? (p. 237). He went on to discuss how exiles would patronize businesses owned by other exiles, which is definitely something the Jewbans did.

I believe the development and continuation of social and human capital to have been critical to the success of this family and of the exile generation in general. American Experience (2005) noted,

> Settling mostly in Miami, but also elsewhere, Cuban Americans have created a wealthy, successful, politically influential immigrant society. As wave upon wave of immigrants rebuilt their lives after the traumatic experience of the revolution, they recreated and reinterpreted Cuban culture in a new homeland, blazing a path that led to the transformation of Miami into a Latin American city. Along with other Latinos— immigrants and U.S. born— they have brought a Latin flavor to American shores.

Having been acquainted with this family for 6½ years, I have picked up what I considered to be signs of their successes. Although all have nice homes and cars, no one is or seemingly was overtly ostentatious. Some of Lilia's cousins, however, are VERY affluent. She has one cousin whose home is on the beach in Miami, and she just listed it for sale for $95 million! In fact, they have all been very welcoming to me and my daughter and generous in inviting us to family affairs and in giving gifts. These are, however, some of the things I have heard about or observed. Jeff mentioned that his mother's family in Cuba must have done "OK" because they had a maid. No one in my family has ever had a maid, at least not that I am aware of! Further, most of David's family has someone who cleans their homes regularly, and Lisette even had a live-in maid. They sometimes refer to her as "Lisette's girl," which I think they mean as a term of endearment but can also reflect that comfort this family has with employing someone to help them at home. She is a lovely woman who they kept on even after the kids were all off to college because she has become part of the family. Again, though, no one in my family has ever employed anyone to clean their homes.

All of the kids had quite expensive Bar and Bat Mitzvahs. Dylans was even held in Israel, which Lilia and Jack attended. We have several metal water bottles with Ethan's initials on them from his Bar Mitzvah, which was held at a local nightclub and included busloads of people. According to Pew Research, only about half of Jews have a Bar or Bat Mitzvah (Pew Research Center, 2021). Lilia says that they never traveled because Jack was too busy running the business, but I have heard mention of Israel several times, Paris, Mexico City, numerous cruises, stays at Marco Island, Florida, and a ranch in central Florida, and more. In contrast, my family took one vacation to Northern Michigan when I was young and then we struggled to get my sister, mom, and me to my aunt's wedding in England when I was in eighth grade. My parents never took a vacation together until after my brother passed away and my sister and I were out of college.

Family events like Jewish holidays are celebrated in a far more lavish way than I was accustomed to. Most of the time they are catered. Outside of a wedding, I don't recall any events my family celebrated being catered. Since David and I have been together, we have attended Stephanie's wedding and his daughter, Rachel B.'s. Both were quite lavish, especially Rachel's, which was held in North Carolina. This stands in stark contrast to our wedding, which, owing to the coronavirus pandemic, was a two-minute affair officiated by a friend (who is a divorce attorney, no less!) in a Waffle House parking lot. Rachel has a large circle of friends from high school and college, all of whom are Jewish (although none Jewban). They all do well economically so have expensive and elaborate birthday parties, bridal showers, bachelor and bachelorette parties, weddings, and baby showers.

Growing up, I knew no one who lived in a gated community. In fact, even as an adult I don't have friends who live in gated communities. Lilia and Jack's home is in one, however, as is Perry's and Lisettes. I consider the ability to afford homes, all of which have pools as well, to be a sign of financial success.

Summer camp is another thing that we were unable to afford but that was a staple for this family and, it seems, among Jews. Pew Research shows that approximately four in ten Jews attended a summer camp when they were young (Pew Research Center, 2021). Jewish summer camps started in the 20th century, when American Jews wanted to get their kids out of the city and into nature as well as to help assimilate them. They became very popular after World War II. Sandra Fox, author of *The Jews of Summer: Summer Camp and Jewish Culture in Postwar America*, explained, "Jews, like many other white Americans in particular, return home from the war. And they receive benefits for veterans of World War II that kind of catapult them into the middle class after decades of building towards that. And in that new middle-class milieu, Jews are moving to American suburbs." Additionally, "The Holocaust had just happened. And so, in the shadow of the Holocaust, American Jews were incredibly anxious about the future of Jewish culture and Judaism as a religion and Jewish summer camps came to be seen as solutions to all kinds of communal ills, but in particular, the problem of assimilation." Jewish summer camps not only helped enhance cultural competence about Judaism and its traditions, but they also tended to have a pro-Israel perspective that might also help explain why this family feels that way (as discussed in Chapter 3). Fox explained, "The idea was basically that Israel was something that could inspire American Jewish kids more than looking towards the Jewish past of oppression and violence in Europe," although some camps did teach about the Holocaust in various ways. David went to "sleepaway camp," as he calls it, as did his siblings and their kids. Most went to a camp that was out of state. The only people I knew who went to summer camp were Girl Scouts and that was usually in the same town or very close to where we lived.

Sunshine Jewelry, the business Jack started with his family that David now runs, once had several retail stores that brought in significant profit. During those days David lived with his ex-wife in a seven-bedroom home they had made in the largely affluent area of Weston, at one point drove a Hummer, and owned several Rolex watches. His parents owned their home, which is worth more than a million, and Lisette lives in a community where the homes are worth multiple millions and neighbors include Miami Dolphins players.

Jeff and Gregg's dad Leon (Leo), Lilia's brother, was a very successful businessman. His first company was Intuero Auto Parts, which he sold twice for significant profit. He was also a real estate developer and investor. I never met him but had heard that he did very well. His son Eric (not interviewed for this book) took over his stone business, Opustone, and Perry worked as CPA of the business. When he passed away in 2021, I attended his service at the Jewish cemetery where the family is buried in Miami. Much to my shock, the musician Billy Joel showed up. David explained to me that Billy Joel had bought his uncle's house and the two became good friends. After the service there was a memorial at

Leo's "man cave," a huge showroom space full of vintage cars and motorcycles that are worth millions.

Natan Rok was also extremely successful. The son of Sara and Jaime Shapiro (Lilia's uncle and his wife), he and his wife Rosita and their three children emigrated from Cuba in 1964. They moved with their parents Isaac & Berta Berezdivin and Salomon & Adela Rok. After working for a short time in the "shmattah" (cheap clothing) business with his Uncle Peisach Rok, he opened a men's clothing business on Flagler Street in Miami. He then bought other stores and real estate on the same street. His son Sergio joined the business in 1983 and they grew it into a retail empire. Rok became the largest property owner in downtown Miami, and the State of Florida re-named Flager Street Natan Rok Boulevard after him. Additionally, the family was very involved with Hillel and Beth Torah synagogue. When Natan and Rosita's son Benny died in a tragic car accident at age 21, the family named Beth Torah Benny Rok Campus in 1983 in his memory. They also established the Rok Family Shul—Chabad Downtown Jewish Center to bring Jewishness and Yiddishkeit to the young families in the Brickell area. I definitely do not have family members with roads, cultural centers, or schools named after them!

RISK-TAKING

Risk-taking and entrepreneurialism were brought up by most of the interviewees. For example, the story of Issac swallowing a diamond while leaving Cuba, an act that could have landed him in prison, showed the willingness to take a risk so as to help provide for his family. Perry explained the success of the Jewbans in South Florida this way: "To be honest, I think a lot has to do with a common struggle. A we are in this together attitude. Jews in general tend to be very entrepreneurial in general and throughout history have done a good job of "figuring it out." The Cuban part gives it a flavor but the root I think is more a Jewish thing." Gregg commented his grandfather's innovation, as he sold 18 karat gold items at their jewelry store in New York before that was popular. Rachel S. explained that in the family, the focus was always on career, business, and money. Education was not presented as being necessary although Jewish education was very important. Rather, success was and is measured largely financially. She believes that the family's history as merchants and being self-sufficient has helped the Jewbans thrive today. Gregg reiterated that. He said that his dad essentially had disdain for education, although the kids were encouraged to go to college. The most important value was making money, however. He expressed that the family narrative is that their success was due to their entrepreneurial spirit and ability to start again. Similarly, Jodi explained that while she and Perry supported their kids' education, in her generation making money was more important. She went to some college and wanted to study Special Education but was told her parents would not pay for it because that career did not make money. She ended up working in a bank before staying home with their children, which was an acceptable option for females, but it was also what she wanted. Jeff explained that their grandparents were all entrepreneurial with various businesses in their lifetimes, including in Eastern Europe, Cuba, and the US. Both Enrique and Dylan noted that few occupations were available to Jews centuries ago, so they had to be entrepreneurs. Enrique also expressed that the family did not see education as a steppingstone to success. Instead, it was typical to leave businesses to sons. Jeff is Leo's oldest son and had a tough relationship with him in later years because he was expected to take over the business and did not want to do so. American Experience (2005) noted that the exile generation was entrepreneurial, but also mentioned assistance in the form of small business loans for Cubans. "Character loans, dispensed by the Republican Bank, and especially by a Cuban banker named Luis Botifoll, allowed Cubans to start small businesses. Applying the entrepreneurial skills brought from their native Cuba and taking advantage of the growing Cuban population in Miami, little by little they created the Miami success story for which Cuban Americans have become known."

Yet, despite this family's emphasis that money mattered more than education, everyone after the exile generation went to college. They were also able to go to whatever colleges they wanted, not those that offered them the most financial aid or scholarships. Pew Research has found that Jews are the most educated population worldwide. Globally, Jews average 13.4 years of school and the majority go on to higher education (Sherwood, 2016)

Although it did come up, the narrative of success does not seem to focus on family support, although that has been consistent across the generations. However, Ester did explain that the business owned by the Shapiros and the Garmizos was essentially started with her mother's dowry while Gregg explained collaboration with family was a factor. Dylan said that their success is due to their Jewishness, which includes knowing that your family will help and being expected to do the same with your kids. While all of the second and third generations went to college, no one mentioned that it was their families that paid for it so none of them has any student debt. This is amazing and definitely not the norm for families in the US. It is obviously much easier to take risks if you know you have family who can assist you if things go awry.

Additionally, as Diner (2015) explained, centuries of global migration prepared Jews for the business of trade and liberated them from the toil and challenges of farming, which was a primary occupation for other immigrant groups around the world. Several interviewees mentioned that Jews were not historically allowed in certain professions, so they had to innovate. While it is true that there have been limitations placed on Jews, Diner (2015) explained, "Counter to the notion that Jews turned to trade because anti-Jewish restrictions prevented them from doing anything else, it in fact liberated them from agriculture, from its unpredictability and its rootedness in a single and fixed place. Likewise, in numerous times and places, trade actually protected the Jews. Jews brought goods to towns, regions, principalities, and nations, enriching the coffers of the state, and extending credit.

In most places, this ensured that the Jews would be allowed to stay, even if they had no formal rights" (p. 131). Further, Diner (2015) noted,

> Explanations that see trade as liberating for the Jews rather than as the negative result of discrimination have also emphasized the absence of any distrust of business and material acquisition within their religious system. Jews traded because they could. Judaism mandated universal male literacy in Hebrew and not coincidentally trade required the ability to read and write, as well as to do sums, keep account books, calculate percentages, even know something about world geography. Throughout the Jewish world, over the course of centuries, young people grew up with trade all around them. They breathed in the idea, almost from the air around them, learning from life itself that business defined everyday existence. Since trade depended upon numeracy, literacy, and linguistic flexibility, young people entered adulthood knowing with a degree of certainty that they would trade. To them, the circumstances of the Jews made business seem just the normal and expected thing to do, whether they entered the field among the lucky few at the higher rungs or the more typical masses who inhabited the lower ones, including the peddlers (p. 132)

Over time, most regions developed restrictions on Jewish peddling, limited what they could trade, where they could do it, and when they could do it. These restrictions forced Jews to innovate and take risks. Diner (2015) explained, "Jews had to experiment with new items, new modes of commerce, and develop those activities not covered by the law. This kind of dealing in novelty, and indeed the act of going out on the road and selling directly to people so different than themselves, involved a degree of risk. Peddling involved, in fact, all kinds of risks" (p. 137–138). Trade also required Jews to be competent communication with different people and across different languages—a valuable form of social capital. Several interviewees noted similar observations about how the family had to innovate as they started anew in Cuba and then in the US.

Muller (2011) asserted that understanding modern Judaism requires considering the development of capitalism. He said, "Capitalism and the Jews" is a subject that makes some people nervous. But you can't properly understand the modern history of the Jews without thinking about the links between Jews and capitalism. And there is a good deal that you can learn about the social, cultural, and political dynamics of capitalism by paying attention to the case of the Jews (p. 7). Further, Muller (2011) located the Jewish emphasis on money not in anything specific to Judaism but rather as a condition of marginalization. He explained that "social exclusion and diasporic circumstances are the key factors in accounting for why Jews have tended to be drawn to the money aspects of the economy" (p. 12). According to Muller (2011), "Jews have been disproportionately involved in the entrepreneurial functions of creating new products, finding new markets for existing products, and pioneering new modes of sales and distribution. Many modern capitalist institutions, while not entirely or even primarily created by Jews, have had a disproportionate number of Jews as entrepreneurial innovators (p. 13). He, like Diner (2015) pointed to the development of human and social capital as key factors that shaped Jewish entrepreneurial success. Ester commented that capitalism comes easily to Jews, especially those like her family with tight family connections. Leo, Jeff, and Gregg's father, always emphasized to them that it was about who you knew, not what you knew.

Noel Shapiro, one of Consuelo's brothers, immigrated from Cuba in 1960, where he had a successful hardware store. His parents Leizer and Berta had run a general shop and they sent Noel to boarding school. As soon as he graduated he opened the store, at just 18 years old. Shapiro, his wife and children, his parents, and his brother and his wife and children all left their houses and businesses behind in the summer of 1960. Shapiro explained that they went as a group and stayed together to help minimize expenses. He tried to find work in hardware stores when they first landed in Miami but could not get hired, as there were so many Cubans were doing the same thing. He got a stroke of good luck when he came across a hardware store called Barry James, which he described as a mini-Home Depot. In his broken English he introduced himself to the lady working inside, and said he needed work. She was crying and saying that her husband had just died, and she did not know how she was going to run the business. Although he had no money, he offered to gradually buy the business from her while running the store. He would take enough money out to support his family and the rest would go to her. The widow consulted with the family and agreed to the deal. Shapiro commented, "I had the guts to make her that proposition. It took me eight and a half years to pay off the amount we agreed to: $70,000." As the store thrived, he associated with builders buying appliances for new construction and began to invest in land and buildings. In 1969 he purchased 600 acres of cattle-grazing land in western Palm Beach County. He was planning to raise cattle, but the seller had left him with only sick cows. The vet he worked with had a sugarcane farm, so Shapiro decided to give that a try. As the *Palm Beach Post* (2006) wrote, he "ultimately became a successful sugar cane farmer by seizing opportunities and following them up with hard work, vision, and a positive outlook," according to his family and fellow sugarcane farmers. Shapiro commented, "This can only happen in the U.S. because of the opportunities offered to people. Anything you want to do, you can learn." Going on, he explained "I will always try anything I don't know. In a year, I think I am an expert. I'm 150 percent American. An immigrant can come here with nothing, and with ambition, he can succeed" (*Palm Beach Post*, 2006). His grandsons are taking over the business.

WORK ETHIC

Most of the interviewees attributed the success of the Jewbans to work ethic. As was noted, reportedly Jack almost never missed a day at the office, working long hours to grow it to success. Both Eva and Consuelo worked in the business into their 90s. Lilia is 81 and still helps David at the jewelry business. Anita, Jeff, and Gregg all recall Leo and his best friend/business partner Joe Pick sleeping on cots at their auto parts business as they tried to grow it. As described above,

Diner (2015) asserted that Jews have long received their start in the work world as peddlers, and this requires physical labor and a strong work ethic. Further, their experience in peddling helped to build connections, hence human capital.

> The history of Jews and the history of peddling went together across the centuries. From the early modern period into the twentieth century, in nearly every place they lived, some, in fact many, and at times most, of them put packs on their backs or clambered up to take their seats on carts, pulled by draft animals, and set off on countless roads to sell, something. As a lived phenomenon, peddling linked their lives in one part of the world and another. Regardless of geography or time, into the early twentieth century it served as their economic métier and helped define relations within their communities and between them and their non-Jewish neighbors. (Diner, 2015, p. 127)

Although she was writing about Latin Jews in the Northeast, Limonic's (2014) observations are appropriate here, as they shed light on how the dual identity of Jewish and Cuban shapes the immigrant experience and family narratives about success. "They come from countries with deep ties to Catholicism, which permeates public and private lives in Latin America. As a result, Jews in Latin America have a strong sense of Jewishness and are often immersed in vibrant and strong communities. At the same time, Jews in Latin America hold prominent positions in the media, academy, business, and government" (pp. 2–3). Further, she explained,

> Even though they face some constraints, my research also suggests that their high socio-economic status and their phenotypic resemblance to the white majority allow members of this group considerable fluidity and choice, and as a result they are able (in certain contexts) to call upon different ethnic identities and establish useful connections, obtain preferential treatment, access established networks, and benefit from policies that promote diversity. Latino Jews are buffered from much of the racial discrimination that affects the life chances of darker-skinned Latinos with less human capital. As a result of their high socio-economic status and phenotypic similarities to the mainstream, Latino Jews are able to benefit from their different ethnic identities—Latino, Jewish or Jewish-Latino and, in fact, their access to different ethnic and ethno-racial groups may influence their prospects for upward mobility (p. 4).

In this family, the same is true in that they (all but Stephanie) appear White so have not suffered the racial discrimination that other Latino immigrants often experience, including later waves of Cubans. Yet they were also able to benefit, as Chapter 3 noted, from identifying as Hispanic when it came to preferential treatment in college admissions.

ON RESILIENCE

Many of my interviewees commented not just about working hard and taking risks but also on accepting challenges and even failures, especially when it came to business endeavors. This is consistent with what Muller (2011) wrote about capitalist successes and the Jews. "In a dynamic capitalist economy, long-term success is a function not only of getting into a potentially rising business at the right time, but also a readiness to get *out* of a declining business or sector before you go bankrupt" (p. 21). Lisette commented that the family success is related to their Jewishness, that's part of why Jews have been hated and discriminated against. They thrive, they are tenacious and work hard, they are educated. Jeff described the family's success as being due to history. He noted that their grandparents did not have many work options, so they had to be entrepreneurs. This involves taking risks, failing, and trying new things. He also observed that they never worked for anyone else. His dad was involved in a number of businesses before the one that made him very successful. But, Jeff noted, rather than purely a self-made man, he did get money from his dad to start that business. He notes that he and his siblings Gregg and Eric all benefitted from his fathers' business success. Part of the resilience is knowing they have family and community to rely on when things are challenging. Limonic (2014) discussed the assimilation and upward mobility of second generation immigrants, "whose parents have high levels of human capital, or who have access to ethnic networks that can buffer them or their children from downward mobility and also provide employment within an ethnic enclave, where according to Wilson and Portes, immigrants can do better than working for similar white-owned business" (p. 21). Limonic (2014) also observed that religion can help immigrants and their children develop social capital that contributes to resiliency and success. "Ethnic churches can also be a factor in upward mobility, through skill building classes for immigrants and the second generation. Additionally, ethnic congregations can act to buffer immigrant children from negative associations linked to downward mobility by offering church sponsored spaces for activities and socialization" (p. 38). While no one in this family is currently very involved with a synagogue or Jewish cultural center, they were when David and his siblings were younger.

CONCLUSION

As is clear from this chapter, there are many reasons for the success of David's family and of Jewbans more broadly. These include having strong family and community connections that can build and sustain social capital, as well as obtaining education (whether it be formal, religious, or vocational). Additionally, being willing to take risks, work hard, and endure difficult times contributes to success. It is important to note, however, that many immigrants also do those things and due to racism and lack of support are unable to achieve as much financially. Further, as is taken up in greater detail in Chapter 5, Cuban immigrants in the exile era were the beneficiaries of several advantages or privileges not afforded to other immigrant groups that also should be considered when discussing their successes. Only Ester commented on this, however, demonstrating that it is not part of the family narrative. Perhaps it should be? If others knew about the privileges Cubans had that helped shape their success perhaps they would have different positions on immigration and supports for immigrants today. As Powell (2022) wrote, the rapid success of the exiles

> was due to an unusual convergence of favorable conditions, some by chance, but some from deliberate policy choices made in Washington: the large number of educated refugees from Cuba's upper and middle classes; preferential treatment under US immigration and nationalization laws; the fact that almost all were considered White in race-conscious America; and bountiful government aid (p. 253).

REFERENCES

American Experience. (2005). Cuban exiles in America. *PBS*. https://www.pbs.org/wgbh/americanexperience/features/castro-cuban-exiles-america/

Burstein, P. (2007). Jewish educational and economic success in the United States. A search for explanation. *Sociological Perspectives, 50*(2), 209–228.

Diner, J. (2015). Peddlers, the great Jewish migration, and the riddle of economic success. In Greenspoon, L. (Ed.), *Wealth and poverty in the Jewish tradition* (pp. 127–149). Purdue University Press.

Limonic, L. (2014). *The privileged "in-between" status of Latino Jews in the Northeastern United States*. Dissertation for City University of New York. https://academicworks.cuny.edu/gc_etds/64

Palm Beach Post. (2006, October 16). Noel Shapiro: Sugarcane farmer has knack for success. Author. https://www.tmcnet.com/usubmit/2006/10/16/1984818.htm

Pew Research Center. (2021, May 11). Jewish Americans in 2020. https://www.pewresearch.org/religion/2021/05/11/economics-and-well-being-among-u-s-jews/#:~:text=As%20a%20whole%2C%20U.S.%20Jews,U.S.%20households%20at%20that%20level.

Sherwood, H. (2016, December 13). Jews are world's best educate religious group, study reveals. *The Guardian*. https://www.theguardian.com/world/2016/dec/13/jews-are-worlds-best-educated-religious-group-study-reveals

CHAPTER 5

IDEALIZED PRE-REVOLUTIONARY CUBA

To hear my husband's extended family and most of the Jewbans I interviewed, Cuba was the best place on earth until that awful Communist Castro took power. It was a land of great beauty, opportunity, friendly people, and lacking discrimination and antisemitism until Castro took that all away So, they say. This is similar to what Perez (2013) found in her interviews with exiles (albeit non-Jews).

Few I interviewed had ever been to Cuba, while only one of the exiles had returned in 60 years. Only two others—one second and one third generation—had visited. Thus, the exiles' view of the island, and the stories they told, were formed partly through nostalgia. Further, the social, cultural, economic, and political position of the Cuban Jews likely slanted their views on Cuba's perfection pre-Castro. The slightly rose-colored glasses about the perfection of pre-revolutionary Cuba also shaped their feelings and beliefs about post-revolutionary Cuba, the reasons people left both immediately after and in subsequent waves, and about social, cultural, and political issues in Cuba immediately post-revolution and today. These feelings and beliefs were passed along the generations, creating an idealized image of Cuba that is not quite accurate.

Shiksa Speaks: A White, Non-Jew's Understanding of the
Cuban Jewish Diaspora and Its Legacy, 81–95.
Copyright © 2025 *Laura Finley*
Published under exclusive licence by Emerald Publishing Limited
HB: 978-1-83708-494-4, PB: 978-1-83708-495-1, ePDF: 978-1-83708-496-8

The reality, according to historical texts, is somewhat different than the narratives I was told. Cuba at that time was indeed one of the most advanced and successful countries in Latin America. Havana was described as a glittery city, with the economy largely fueled by sugar sales to the US and tourism. It ranked fifth in the hemisphere in per capita income, had the third highest life expectancy and was second in ownership of telephones and automobiles. This island had more televisions per inhabitant than any other country in the hemisphere. Its literacy rate was 76 percent—fourth highest in Latin America. Cuba had a relatively advanced medical system, ranking 11th in the world in the number of doctors per capita and had many private clinics and hospitals that served the poor. It was also home to a thriving middle class (American Experience, 2005). In most ways, Cuba mirrored the US in newly popular foods like hamburgers and hotdogs, similar-looking apartments, and hobbies like baseball. Members of the elite drive cars imported from the US and department stores carried largely American fashions and goods. Ricardo "Dick" Morales Jr. told Powell (2022) that in pre-revolutionary Cuba, his family was well-off and that "Cubans were very Americanized. We had bank accounts in New York. All the movies we saw were American movies. The clubs were organized American style. They had English names: Havana Yacht Club, Vedado Tennis Club, the Country Club of Havana, the Biltmore Yacht and Country Club" (p. 5). One example of the prosperity of much of the Cuban Jews was the luxurious Patronato de la Casa de la Communidad Hebrea de Cuba (Bet h-Keneset ha-Gadol), which was constructed in 1953 in Vedado and funded largely by the affluent Ashkenazi (Levine, 2010).

Lilia described Cuba as beautiful—a paradise, she calls it. In fact, as I finish writing this, we had a conversation where she repeatedly said "life was perfect." She and her friends would spend time at the beaches, and everyone hung out at the Patronato, which she described as being like a country club for Jews. Neither she nor Jack ever returned, and she said she never would. Enrique echoed those sentiments. He also referred to pre-revolutionary Cuba as nearly perfect. He said that he had seen photos of his old school and other places that were important to him growing up and that he did not want to remember them so worn down as he believes them to be today, a situation he attributed to the Castro regime. Ester was only a child when her family left Cuba and she also recalls its beauty, as does her sister Rachel S., who remembers with fondness eating Cuban foods like plantain chips and mangoes sold by street vendors. Interestingly, none mentioned how Americanized pre-revolutionary Cuba had become. The impression they give, and that they gave to their children and grandchildren, was of a unique tropical paradise. This is true of many exiles, as most were middle or upper class so had good lives in Cuba. For example, one of the people Powell (2022) interviewed explained that in Cuba they a maid, chauffer, gardener, laundress, and cook and the family routinely went to the country club or to their vacation home in Varadero.

The narrative passed along the generations is that these positive images and experiences, all that were wrecked by the revolution. But many Cuban Jews actually supported the revolution at first. This is largely omitted from the family narrative except for Ester. She once wrote about it, describing a conversation with her cousin after the family emigrated to Miami.

> One month into our 'vacation' at the seedy Tropics hotel, my cousin Edith corrected me during the course of play when I mentioned Castro, as we always had, in reverential, heroic terms. Edith commented casually, with her customary older cousin's air of condescending superiority: 'You are wrong, Ester Rebeca, Castro is bad, es malo, it is because of him that we have left Cuba, and can never go back.' That moment joined the secret collection of shattering and unexaminable contradictions which I began to hoard during my life as an exile (Rok, 1995, p. 89).

Yet, for others, the island was not so perfect in the pre-Castro eras. Yes, Havana was an international city. Yes, the island had more Cadillacs than anywhere in the world. Its Tropicana's cabaret was the most luxurious in the world, regularly featuring such US performers as Rita Hayworth, Nat King Cole, and Duke Ellington. But these treasures came with a sidekick—organized crime. As Levine (2010) wrote, "criminals, some on the run from the United States, infiltrated Havana's entertainment industry" (p. 203). Many mobsters from the US funneled dirty money into Cuba and used the island to escape the reach of the FBI and IRS as well as other entities. It was used to build casinos and hotels, which in turn generated the funds used to facilitate the corrupt political system led by President Fulgencio Batista. In 1946 what was basically a mafia convention was held at the historic Hotel Nacional. Within months of Batista's 1952 coup, mobster Mayer Lansky purchased a partnership in the Cabaret Montmartre, and President Batista asked him during the winter season of 1953–54 to "clean up the casino industry." This meant building a gambling wing on the premier hotel in Vedado, the Hotel Nacional. Lansky then built his own hotel, the Riviera, which was the largest casino hotel in the world outside of Las Vegas (Levine, 2010, p. 203). Crooner Frank Sinatra, whose career was supported by the US mafia, was friends with Lucky Luciano, and was used as a draw to Cuba's hotels, nightclubs, and casinos. Politicians were also known to frequent the island, often to hire prostitutes. In the 1950s, Cuba was the gambling mecca of the world. It was the number one draw in the Caribbean and, according to UNLV Professor Tony Henthorne, it was "built as America's playground." Under Batista, famed mob man Meyer Lansky was Chief Gaming Officer, and their goal was to make the island "like Vegas on steroids." Luciano, Trafficante Jr., and Dino Cellini, all moved to Cuba during the Kefauver investigations in the 1950s. While serving as a Senator, John F. Kennedy, with Florida Senator George Smathers, took a visit to the island. Mobster Santo Trafficante helped set up a tryst with three Cuban prostitutes in a hotel room. Unbeknownst to the politicians, Trafficante and an associate had set up a two-way mirror through which they watched the orgy (Worrall, 2016).

Records show that the Cuban Jews largely accepted the graft on the island, as it was generally good for business. Fellow Jewban Anders (2005) said that her father knew Cuba as "a corrupt place under the crooked, ruthless dictator General Fulgencio Batista's rule, and corrupt before him, but it was an alluring, sexy, prosperous, lush, advanced, beguiling, laissez-faire kind of corrupt. You know, fun corrupt" (p. 25). As noted in Chapter 1, no one I interviewed mentioned organized crime at all. Either they were unaware or simply accepted it as normal and not worthy of mention. The influence of organized crime was not so good for others, though. In protest of anything Batista, Cubans ransacked the casinos and Castro prohibited gambling. These changes were a boon for Las Vegas, as it no longer had the competition presented by Cuba (Bethencourt, 2022).

It was this idyllic narrative that Castro's revolutionaries criticized. They described the island as "the brothel of the Western hemisphere." Many went poor and hungry while the elite prospered and the government catered to American tourists who frequented its luxurious hotels, casinos, and basked in its sunny beaches (American Experience, 2005). Brothels also abound in Havana, as did jai alai frontons, racetracks, restaurants, and resorts, all of which encouraged and increased tourism. Cockfighting and illegal lotteries were common as well. Havana was described as a welcoming and easy place to live—at least for all but the lower classes. For example, most middle- and upper-class families had maids whom they treated patronizingly. Behar (1995, p. 2) commented on how these competing narratives about Cuba persist today and how they shape current views about the island.

> Cuba since the revolution has been imagined as either a utopia of a backward police state. Cuba, viewed with utopian eyes, is a defiant little island that has dared to step on the toes of a great superpower and dreamed ambitiously of undoing the legacy of poverty, inequality, and unfulfilled revolutions that has plagued Latin America and the Caribbean. Alternately, as newspaper headlines in the U.S. media like to declare, Cuba is 'an island of lost souls,' a place where 'huddled masses yearn for the comforts of life' and will sacrifice everything to leave, plunging into the 'deadly sea of dreams' as *balseros* (raft people)or Cuban 'wetbacks.' Within this conflicting web or representations born of the Cold War, there is little room for a more nuances and complex vision of how Cubans on the island and in the diaspora give meaning to their lives, their identity, and their culture in the aftermath of a battle that has split the nation at the root.

As Parker (2015, p. iii) wrote,

> As the largest island in the Caribbean, Cuba boasts beautiful scenery, as well as a rich and diverse culture. Yet, throughout Cuban history, the beauty of this famous socialist nation has been marred by social inequalities, primarily affecting class, gender, and race." Historical records show profound inequalities pre-Castro, especially between Whites and Blacks and city and country dwellers. Nearly all who resided in the rural parts of country, outside of the sugar plantation owners, resided in dismal poverty. Their work was largely seasonal, so the sugarcane cutters—the macheteros—were nearly always in debt, hungry and malnourished. The healthcare and educational systems typically did not reach them, so illiteracy was the norm.

Those who did get to attend school usually did not make it past first or second grade (American Experience, 2005).

Ester is the only one who emphasized that things might not have been so ideal for all people in pre-revolutionary Cuba. This, she asserted, was likely due to the fact that the Cuban Jews lived, worked, and went to school with mostly other Cuban Jews, and those they knew in Havana were mostly middle class and all-White. Therefore, they were not really situated to see some of the racism or classism that did exist. Further, they were taught that some degree of gender equality was normal, "how men and women are supposed to behave," and homophobia was also quite normalized and therefore went unquestioned by most at the time and to this day amongst many of the Jewbans.

ANTISEMITISM IN PRE-REVOLUTIONARY CUBA

The exiles had been told stories about antisemitism in Eastern Europe by their parents, aunts, and uncles. Indeed, all reiterated that this was the primary reason for the exodus that landed them in Cuba, and that is the story that was passed along. Everyone had lost family who waited too long to leave Eastern Europe, as they perished in the camps. But none of the interviewees shared that Cuba too struggled with mistreatment of Jews. Yet historical records show that this antisemitism was happening when the exile's families migrated to Cuba, so the omission of that narrative is interesting. The failure to mention antisemitism in Cuba seems to be due to a variety of factors. First, the exiles I interviewed grew up in the late 1940s and into the 1950s. This was, as described above, a time of general prosperity in Cuba and after World War II and it definitely was for these families, The antisemitism of earlier decades, described below, had basically been replaced by sympathy for Jews and others who died in the Holocaust. Their parents did not mention living on the island when there was antisemitism, perhaps because they wanted to believe the idyllic narrative or because they did not want to discuss anti-Jewish sentiment, wanting it to be a thing from another place and another time.

Despite some records saying Jews did not feel antisemitism in their daily lives, reports from the later 1920s and through World War II indicate that indeed antisemitism existed on the island. In 1928, the Havana City Council banned peddlers. Given that most were Jews, this was clearly aimed at them, and fifteen men were arrested for selling goods at lower prices than established retailers. The global depression and the fall of sugar prices in the 1930s further fueled anti-Jewish sentiment. After Hitler rose to power a group of fascists on the island began to campaign for "Cuba for Cuba and for the Cubans." They pushed for legislation requiring 80 percent of employees be Cuban. It was not passed, but legislation in 1933 did impose a 50 percent Cuban requirement for employers. Nazi sympathizers organized to create a campaign to Nazify Cuba. Some of the press distributed anti-Jewish material and accused Jews of being communist sympathizers. Jews also faced physical attacks and assaults on their businesses. Joseph Goebbels sent

Nazi agents to the island to disseminate antisemitic literature and pro-Nazi materials. Juan Prohias, founder of the Cuban Nazi Party, hosted a daily "antisemitic hour" on one of the radio stations. Cuban merchants of Spanish origin also engaged in antisemitic rhetoric, as they feared the new Jews posed a challenge to their retail businesses. Interestingly, the concern was more about Polish Jews, who were considered by many to have "unscrupulous" business practices (Glaser, 2015).

Jews could not become citizens until the later 1930s, although reportedly it was easy to purchase illegal birth certificates. The early 1930s saw a surge in antisemitism in Cuba, much of it coming from European propaganda. For instance, several newspapers and radio programs called for a halt in Jewish immigration to the island, referring to the Jews from Europe as "human garbage." Tensions were reduced as the economy picked up, and Jewish businesses began to thrive. In fact, Levine (2010) asserts that Cuban Jewish companies held 60 percent share of all clothing, fabric, and shoe manufacturing and this helped reduce Cuban dependence on outside suppliers and the effects of the Great Depression.

Subsequent to the St, Louis incident described in Chapter 1, thousands of Jews still did end up in Cuba but not legally, therefore they remained in a limbo state, unable to work and therefore waiting for the war to end. Eastern European Jews who had previously emigrated were hostile toward German Jewish refugees and complained about any relief efforts they received. Antisemitism continued on the island. Some of this was codified in the Cuban Constitution that was written in 1939–1940. One provision prohibited immigrants from practicing law or medicine, and another forbade entry to refugees for political or religious purposes. It took effect in 1940 with the presidency of Fulgencio Batista. Although he reportedly had many Jewish friends, he did not do much to contest the anti-Semitic propaganda although he did outlaw the Cuban Nazi and fascist parties (Levine, 2010).

RACISM IN PRE-REVOLUTIONARY CUBA

When asked about racism, the narrative is that pre-revolutionary Cuba was way better than the United States and that people were treated equally. Only Ester and Enrique expressed that yes, there was racism, but it looked different than the stark segregation of the US that still existed in the early 1960s when they all arrived. She knows this because she has studied the history of Cuba and has also visited the island, unlike the others. She expressed that while housing segregation like that in the US was not a significant issue, people of color generally had their own social, cultural, and religious groups, as did Jews. Enrique also recalls that there was racism—certain clubs would not allow Blacks, Jews, or the lower classes, for instance. Like Ester, he noted that the Jews self-segregated, and recalls one street in Cuba that was all Jewish shops, largely garments. He said he went to City College of New York and groups self-segregated there as well.

In part the failure to notice racism may be due to the fact that these exiles all lived in Havana, rather than in the more rural parts of Cuba, where racism was more obvious. Further, as noted above, they lived, worked, and socialized largely with other White Ashkenazi Jews. Although they did not refer to it as racism, many of the interviewees noted that there were tensions between the Ashkenazi and Sephardic Jews in Cuba. While many factors were involved in those tensions, it is undeniable that the Ashkenazi were largely White, and the Sephardic were generally darker skinned.

As was noted in Chapter 1, the Cuban economy had long been based on slavery, as had that of its neighbor the US. And, like the US, the legacy of racism persisted and remains persistent. Cuba was the "agro-industrial graveyard" of sugar and coffee production. This term was used because slavery in Cuba was basically a death sentence: most enslaved Africans died within a few years of being transported to the island. These atrocious death rates meant that slavery persisted, as more slaves were always needed. At least 85 percent of the slaves brought to Cuba were transported after the US and England banned slaver in 1808 (Chambers, 2015). Parker (2015, p. 21) explained that historical patterns resulted in continued racial and gender disparities in Cuba. "The constant denial of education that was provided to white Cubans segregated Afro-Cubans and women from society, forcing them to remain illiterate and unable to advance socially or economically."

None of the interviewees mentioned that Cuba was involved with the slave trade. When I explained that slavery was an integral part of building both the US and Cuban economies, they seemed shocked. This information was not mentioned by the exiles nor by their progeny or third generation Jewbans. The narrative of Cuba's pre-revolutionary egalitarianism is thus unchallenged in the family, and it seems that the education system has also failed to provide a comprehensive view of pre-and post-revolutionary Cuba (Chambers, 2015).

Data about race pre-revolution can be obtained via the censuses of 1899, 1907, 1919, 1931, and 1943. Modeled after US censuses, however, the data simply classified people as White or non-White so does not offer a nuanced view. The 1953 census data is even less detailed, only publishing the overall racial composition of the population. Nonetheless, the existing data does provide a picture of pre-revolutionary Cuba. de la Fuente (1995) noted that by 1919, the White population reached just over 72 percent and stayed at approximately that percentage for the next 40 years, reaching a high point of 75 percent in 1943. It declined slightly in the 1950s and then again by 1981, with the non-White population being largely mixed race, or mulatto. The increase in the White population until the 1940s was likely due to higher birth rates, lower death rates, and immigration (Hansing, 2018).

As *PBS* noted in its American Experience (2005) episode about Cuba, racism was prominent pre-revolution. Private clubs and beaches were segregated. It was reported that even Batista, who was of mixed race (mulatto) was once denied membership to one of Havana's most exclusive clubs. The differences were most stark between urban and rural Cuba. Racism also blighted Cuban society. "One might best summarize the complex situation by saying that urban Cuba had come to resemble a Southern European country (with a living standard as high or surpassing that of France, Spain, Portugal and Greece) while rural Cuba replicated the conditions of other plantation societies in Latin America and the Caribbean," said analyst Mark Falcoff (American Experience, 2005).

Several of the exiles explained that the Cuban constitution mandated equality, which is true in some respects but not entirely so. The first constitution in 1901, after independence from Spain, did specify that all men had equal rights, but it did not explicitly mention race and thus systemic racism persisted. For instance, while the U.S. occupied the island, Afro-Cuban veterans were barred from many public service positions. Additionally, informal discrimination continued because racial consciousness was considered unpatriotic. It was, therefore, not to be discussed. Given trends in nearby Haiti and the Dominican Republic, fear of Afro-Cuban control was always present in Cuban politics. Immigration policies favored Spain and other European countries over mainly Creole Caribbean populations as way to "whiten" Cuba (Sawyer, 2005). Black political parties were actually banned and in 1912, a protest more than 4,000 Afro-Cubans were massacred by Cuban forces during a protest. The message was clear: Racial uprisings were unacceptable and would be met with the harshest of force (American Experience, 2005).

The Constitution of 1940 promised progressive measures, including full equality between all citizens regardless of race, color, sex, or class and rights of illegitimate children were formally guaranteed. Many portions of the Constitution needed legislative backing to be implemented throughout society, however, and this did not occur. As such, while de jure there was not discrimination, it remained de facto (American Experience, 2005). de la Fuente (1995) also reported that while Cuba had relatively high literacy rates by Latin American standards at the time, the education system was suffering pre-revolution, and its decline was felt far more by non-Whites. Another reason for the decline in literacy in the 1940s and 1950s was the introduction of many private schools, which the Black and poor often could not afford. The exiles interviewed here all went to private Jewish schools and thus were beneficiaries of this trend. Further, none of the interviewees mentioned that the literacy gap completely disappeared by 1981, a result of the revolution's egalitarian approach to education. Non-Whites pre-revolution were significantly underrepresented in higher education, especially in certain specialties, which prevented their access to white collar jobs. Thus, while the government did not specifically discriminate, discrimination resulted in educational barriers that then became labor barriers. A small fraction of Afro-Cubans held teaching and military positions but most hold low-level jobs, including domestic work (Rogers, 2020).

CLASSISM IN PRE-REVOLUTIONARY CUBA

Deep class divides existed before the revolution, even amidst Cuba's heyday. Given that this was the main focus of the revolution, I offer only a few observations here.

In particular, rural people struggled as the sugar boom was waning and there was no reliable economic replacement in sight. Cuba had become increasingly economically dependent on the US. By the late 1950s the US held 90 percent interest in Cuba's mines, 80 percent of its public utilities, 50 percent of its railways, 40 percent of its sugar production, and 25 percent of its bank deposits. Social systems and safety nets were unavailable to Cubans living in rural areas. Only 15 percent of rural residents, for instance, even had running water (Parker, 2015). As Parker (2015, p. 36) expressed, "By all means, life outside of Havana was considered to be a personal hell for rural citizens." While the revolution promised to end inequality (and in many ways did so), Batista's fleeing in the middle of the night with more than $40 million of government funds did not help (Geiling, 2007).

While Cuba's government, mafiosos, and the affluent adored the opulent casinos and nightclubs, they were off limits to most Cubans, especially the poor, who would never have been able to meet the required dress codes or betting limits (Farber, 2015). As is discussed in the next segment, racism, classism, and sexism intersected in pre-revolutionary Cuba. Afro-Cuban women had the fewest options, with many having to turn to sex work to survive (Darko, 2022).

SEXISM IN PRE-REVOLUTIONARY CUBA

In some respects, pre-revolutionary Cuba was progressive on gender equality, especially amongst its Latin American counterparts. The State's rhetoric professed the importance of gender equality and the Communist Party campaigned for equal wages when it was founded in 1925. In 1938 the Communist Party was legalized under the name Partido Socialista Popular (PSP) with a program of equal rights for women and "negroes." Equal pay for equal work was enshrined in the 1940 constitution, although in practice women did not have the opportunity to do "equal work," as they were still relegated to specific, low-paying sectors (Murray, 1979a). Estimates suggest that in 1958, Cuban women made up roughly 13 percent of the workforce, which was higher than many other Latin American countries (Mesa-Lago, 1981; Smith & Padula, 1988).

When asked about sexism, again it was only Ester and her sister Rachel S. of the exiles who noted how women were treated. Ester said that women were treated as if their purpose was to be property. She explained that her mother was the favorite of their grandmother Berta because she was shy and meek, but also wealthy. At the time she married in 1951 her dowry was $10,000, equivalent to approximately $125,000 today. This was used to start a family business that became very successful. Ester also commented that women who defied gender norms were seen as an afront. Consuelo was described as a strong and vivacious woman who was the least favorite of her family. Rachel S. said that their grandmother favored her sons over Tia Consuelo and that in general, sons were favored over daughters. Ester, like Consuelo, was outspoken and sexual and this was not acceptable at the time and especially by this family. Interestingly, the other exiles did not express that sexism was an issue, rather they seemed to imply that it was not because they emphasized that the women in their family all worked in the family businesses. For instance, Eva was noted as the "worker" in her relationship. But a closer read shows that while the women worked, they often did so for no pay, they did not own the businesses, and they had little say or decision-making power. It is not clear if any of the female interviewees who worked in the businesses in Cuba and in the US were actually paid or whether the work was simply accepted. The latter would not be atypical (Farber, 2015). Life was different for rural woman than for urban women in pre-revolutionary Cuba. Rural women typically worked on farms as unpaid labor until they got married. The individuals I interviewed did not have any insight about this, as they were all from Havana.

The narrative told to later generations was that communism is entirely bad, always. But communism, as Ester noted, often improves the lot for women, at least in some respects. This comes from the work of Marx and Engels, who attributed the subordination of women to the emergence of private property in the means of production, as monogamous women were relegated to the domestic sphere and thereby made dependent on male partners. By extension, then, the end to women's subjugation should come when women are allowed to be part of the means of production and thus socialism should benefit women tremendously. Ending the role of women as transactional objects—through sex work or in marriage—was a vision of Marx. Marx and Lenin viewed household work as mundane and philosophized that if these tasks were moved to the public sector instead of the home, women would be free to participate in political and social life (Goldman, 1993).

Yet, too often experiments in socialism have at first advanced women's rights but then relegated women to second class when other issues were perceived as higher priority. For instance, Murray (1979a) explains that women became in control of their own fertility and reproductive freedom in socialist Soviet Union, but economic destruction caused by World War I's decimation of the population shifted priority to building it back up. Regardless of the flaws in this thinking and its implementation, an examination of the stories versus the reality of sexism in pre-revolutionary Cuba is of use.

While these interviewees applauded Cuba's glitzy and fun atmosphere, they did not discuss the reasons for it. In large part, the vibrant tourism of pre-revolutionary Cuba was due to the sexual exploitation of women. Only Ester expressed that objectification was a significant part of the Cuban economy and that it was actually one of the things the revolution targeted. In fact, women's bodies were controlled and manipulated since the colonial days in Cuba (Darko, 2022). As Murray (1979a) noted, "Cuba was a holiday island for Americans, and they expected not only sexual services from the 270 brothels, 100 hotels with rent-by-the-hour rooms, and 700 'bars' which existed in Havana by 1958 (at that time, 0.5% of all Cuban women were prostitutes), but also entertainment at night-clubs and shows which exploited women commercially in 'Americanized' fashion, and they employed Cuban maids and domestic servants to run their country houses" (Murray, 1979a, pp. 60). As noted in Chapter 1, although it is hard to find accurate numbers, estimates of the number of sex workers in 1958 ranged from 25,000 to 100,000. Given that the number of women working in the formal economy was between 200,000 and 290,000, these estimates are staggering (Mesa-Lago, 1981; Smith & Padula, 1996). The ratio of women earning a living from sex work in Cuba approximately double that of New York City at the time (Farber, 2015). Women of color had long been perceived as hypersexual and stigmatized as prostitutes even when they were not. This is due to European traditions of what makes an "honorable woman:" Family respectability, inheritance, and social status (Darko, 2022). Tourism in the 1950s further fetishized and commodified women's bodies, none more than those of women of color.

Although not so true for these more affluent Cuba Jews, big families were indicators of a man's virility, and thus women were encouraged to reproduce. Birth control was perceived as promoting women's infidelity and undermining of men's authority so not promoted nor easily accessible before the revolution. Childcare was the domain of women, and nurseries only available for the wealthy (Murray, 1979b).

Being more affluent and part of a tightknit community of family and friends, childcare was not an issue for the exiles I interviewed. Their grandmothers, aunts, and other relatives took care of kids, which allowed for the women to work in ways that were not available to other women on the island. They worked in family businesses where the children as they grew up also worked, and when they were younger the kids went to Yeshiva. As Ester explained, "A woman's value was in what her body could bring to the highest bidder in terms of who they married, and so many marriages were arranged among the Cuban Jews expressly for that purpose." Even marriages to Sephardic Jews were looked down upon, securing that the community remained especially tight. While they did not emphasize it, the interviewees were all at least middle class in Cuba and thus had maids who were invariably poor women (Farber, 2015). Other research has identified the challenges some who fled Cuba to the US faced living in homes where they were expected to do dishes and clean up, as they were not expected to do so in Cuba with a maid employed. Again, this was not mentioned, but many of the interviewees from all generations do still retain women who clean their homes.

Like other Latin American countries, Cuban men have long been rewarded for exhibiting *machismo*, while women are expected to be *decente*, or honorable and polite (Bettinger-López, 2000). "White Cuban women were also expected to maintain roles that were viewed as "female" and tended to revolve around domestic duties within households. Afro-Cuban women in particular were vastly mistreated and unrecognized as citizens with their own rights and were usually only allowed to serve the households of the elite as slaves. In general, women were given inferior treatment to allow men to be free and rule the island without any opposition" (Parker, 2015, p. 23). These gender role norms emanated from the upper classes and from the influence of the Catholic church. Women are expected to be good wives and mothers. Being single as an adult woman is not honorable, nor is being wild or acting without the supervision of family (Chaney, 1979). Typically, Latin American women had little control over their own lives. Male family members pretty much control the life inside the home and outside of it. *Supermadre*, according to Chaney (1979), is a mother who worked outside the home but in labor based on traditional gender norms in work that supported men and children. Again, only Ester commented on these issues.

While the revolutionaries were far from perfect, they were more likely to actually promote gender equality. Many women were involved in the movement to overthrow Batista, and Castro commented on the importance of women's participation. By 1958 about one twentieth of the Rebel Army's 3000 soldiers were women, although they served largely in "female" roles like nursing, sewing, and cooking. When the Rebels came to power they had no specific plan for gender equality, however. Cuba today is a mixed bag on gender equality, but by many measures is ahead of the US.

HOMOPHOBIA IN PRE-REVOLUTIONARY CUBA

None of the interviewees mentioned homophobia in Cuba, yet history is clear that it was until quite recently a significant problem. Again, only Ester was aware of the changes. In all likelihood, the lack of mention by these interviewees is also due to the fact that they lived in tight communities and did not interact with those who were unlike them, including anyone who was gay or lesbian. LGBTQ individuals at that time, like in the US, were often closeted because it was unsafe for them to be "out" publicly. The second and third generation interviewees are generally politically progressive and profess to support gay rights, although very few have friends or any regular interaction with people who are not heterosexual. Some of the exiles and second generation still use epithets like "*pajaro*" (bird) to describe flamboyant gay males or even worse, "*maricon*" (faggot). They have been corrected by their children and grandchildren.

In pre-Revolutionary Cuba, the gay community was relegated to the few LGBT-friendly bars in Havana. Strict laws criminalized homosexuality and gay men were targeted for harassment. In 1938, Cuba enacted the Public Ostentation Law as part of Cuba's Penal Code. It did not explicitly outlaw homosexuality, but it prohibited display of "public homosexual behavior." While the 1940 constitution stated the right to equality, it did not specifically address gay rights. American tourists also reinforced patriarchal, heterosexuality as the norm (Halatyn, 2012).

There were LGBTQ individuals in rural areas and because they were so small, it was even easier to identify and ostracize the few people who did not fit the compulsory heterosexuality that the machismo dominated culture assumed. The reality was that most LGBTQ individuals felt pressure to remain closeted at risk of public persecution, police harassment, loss of work, and more (Figueroa, 2022). Many in the LGBTQ community felt that the revolution would improve their lives, but Castro's promises of egalitarianism did not extend to gay rights. The new administration continued to enforce the Public Ostentation Law and gay men were routinely harassed and imprisoned in harsh labor camps.

Risech (1995, p. 62) commented on the deeply engrained homophobia on the island, both before the revolution, during it, and for some time thereafter.

> The fossilized rhetoric of *Anorada Cuba*, the lament for a pre-Castro Cuba that never really existed, a mythical Cuba where everyone had wealth, health, and high culture, where there was no racism, was the constant refrain at the dinner table. Always in counterpoint was the theme of the communist evil which had despoiled our island paradise, often punctuated with allusions to Fidel's perfidiousness and his brother Raul's supposed homosexuality. From these representations I drew the following lessons: it was bad to be a communist, it was worse to be a *maricon*, and it was *el como* (the ultimate sin) to be both. It would be years before I would discover that being *maricon* had anything to do with sex, but the link between communism and queerness—then defined more me as effeminacy—was clear enough.

Today, Cuba is far more supportive of gay rights and in many ways is ahead of the US. In 2022, the island enacted a new Family Code establishing not just gay marriage but the right of gay couples to adopt. This represents a legislative change but also a change in attitude for much of the country, although there was opposition by Cuba's Catholic Church. TV, radio and newspaper coverage plus billboards and parades sponsored by the Community party promoted the referendum (Acosta & Rios, 2022).

CONCLUSION

Why does this matter, one might ask? For one, the failure to consider that Cuba was imperfect before the revolution coupled with the notion that the revolution ruined everything seems to result in a disdain for anything Cuba today. As Eckstein (2009) explained, exiles remained virulently anti-Castro, despite having a distorted construction of the country and what happened post revolution. Additionally, the plight of Jews as a victimized group was emphasized by these interviewees and is a theme found in other research about the Jewish diaspora in Cuba and elsewhere. The Jewbans view their lives in Cuba—and pass along the stories—through rose-colored glasses and exaggerate the victimization they experienced under Castro's Cuba. The social issues Cuba struggled with during its pre-revolutionary heyday were more frequently experienced by the poor and people of color—most Jewbans were not. Rather, they were middle and upper class and White, especially those who left in the early days after the revolution, as did the exiles I interviewed.

Cubans in South Florida have for decades been a powerful voting bloc. Most exiles and even later generations vote Republican, as the Republican party is quick to denounce anything it can label "socialist" or "communist," the naughty words to Cuban Americans. This is true of many of the people I interviewed, although they represent more political diversity that many Cuban Americans. Their re-narrated memories of Cuba and the stories they tell shape how they vote today. The story of victimization omits the many privileges that were given to Cuban emigres, some of which persist today. The issues of privilege afforded to Cuba emigres and Jewbans' feelings toward Cuba today are the topics of Chapters Six and Seven.

REFERENCES

Acosta, N., & Rios, A. (2022, November 14). *Cuba welcomes gay rights as progressive family code takes hold.* Reuters. https://www.reuters.com/world/americas/cuba-welcomes-gay-rights-progressive-family-code-takes-hold-2022-11-14/

American Experience. (2005). Pre-Castro Cuba. *PBS.* https://www.pbs.org/wgbh/americanexperience/features/comandante-pre-castro-cuba/

Anders, G. (2005). *Jubana! The awkwardly true and dazzling adventures of a Jewish Cubana goddess.* Rayo.

Behar, R. (1995). Introduction. In R. Behar (Ed.), *Bridges to Cuba/Puentes a Cuba* (pp. 1–20). University of Michigan Press.

Bethencourt, A. (2022, October 10). *The rise of Vegas, thanks to the fall of Cuba.* KTNV. https://www.ktnv.com/positivelylv/the-rise-of-vegas-thanks-to-the-fall-of-cuba

Bettinger-López, C. (2000). *Cuban-Jewish journeys: Searching for identity, home, and history in Miami.* University of Tennessee Press.

Chambers, S. (2015, September 27). *Our forgotten slavery horror: The shameful, untold history of America and the Cuban slave trade.* Salon. https://www.salon.com/2015/09/27/our_forgotten_slavery_horror_the_shameful_untold_history_of_america_and_the_cuban_slave_trade/

Chaney, E. (1979). *Supermadre: Women in politics in Latin America.* The University of Texas Press.

Darko, C. (2022). Postcards from paradise: How Cuba's tourism industry enabled the hypersexualization of Black women and erasure of female Afro-Cuban identity. *Of Life and History, 3*(7), 1–15.

de la Fuente, A. (1995). Race and inequality in Cuba, 1899–1981. *Journal of Contemporary History, 30*(1), 131–168.

Eckstein, S. (2009). *The immigrant divide: How Cubans changes the US and their homeland.* Routledge.

Farber, S. (2015. September). Cuba before the revolution. *Jacobin.* https://jacobin.com/2015/09/cuban-revolution-fidel-castro-casinos-batista

Figueroa, C. (2022). Rice and beans with a side of queer: Sociolegal developments in the Cuban LGBTQ+ community. *William & Mary Journal of Race, Gender, and Social Justice, 28*(2), 421–443. https://scholarship.law.wm.edu/cgi/viewcontent.cgi?article=1576&context=wmjowl

Geiling, N. (2007). Before the revolution. *Smithsonian.* https://www.smithsonianmag.com/history/before-the-revolution-159682020/

Glaser, Z. (2015). *Refugees and relief: The American Jewish Joint Distribution Committee and European Jews in Cuba and Shanghai, 1938–1943.* Dissertation for City University of New York. https://academicworks.cuny.edu/cgi/viewcontent.cgi?article=1560&context=gc_etds

Goldman, W. (1993). *Women, the state, and revolution: Soviet family policy and social life, 1917–1936.* Cambridge University Press.

Halatyn, J. (2012, October 24). *From persecution to acceptance: The history of LGBT rights in Cuba.* Council on Hemispheric Affairs. https://coha.org/from-persecution-to-acceptance-history-of-lgbt-in-cuba/

Hansing, K. (2018). Race and rising inequality in Cuba. *Current History, 117*(796), 69–72.

Levine, R. (2010). *Tropical diaspora: The Jewish experience in Cuba.* Markus Weiner Publishers.

Mesa-Lago, C. (1981). *The economy of Socialist Cuba.* University of New Mexico Press.

Murray, N. (1979a). Socialism and feminism: Women and the Cuban revolution, part 1. *Feminist Review, 2,* 57–73.

Murray, N. (1979b). Socialism and feminism: Women and the Cuban revolution, part 2. *Feminist Review, 3,* 99–108.

Parker, A. (2015). Race and inequality in Cuban tourism during the 21st century. Thesis for California State University, San Bernardino. https://scholarworks.lib.csusb.edu/cgi/viewcontent.cgi?article=1231&context=etd&httpsredir=1&referer=

Perez, R. (2013). Paradise lost: Older Cuban American exiles' ambiguous loss of leaving the homeland. *Journal of Gerontological Social Work, 56*(7), 599–622.

Powell, D. (2022). *Ninety miles and a lifetime away: Memories of early Cuban exiles.* University of Florida Press.

Risech, F. (1995). Political and cultural cross-dressing: Negotiating a second-generation Cuban American identity. In R. Behar (Ed.), *Bridges to Cuba/Puentes a Cuba* (pp. 57–71). University of Michigan Press.

Rogers, J. (2020). *Women in socialist Cuba: Political and economic equality.* James Madison University Senior Thesis Project, https://commons.lib.jmu.edu/cgi/viewcontent.cgi?article=1071&context=honors202029

Rok, E. (1995). Finding what had been lost in plain view. In R. Behar (Ed.), *Bridges to Cuba/Puentes a Cuba* (pp. 85–985). University of Michigan Press.

Sawyer, M. (2005). *Racial politics in post-revolutionary Cuba.* Cambridge University Press.

Smith, L., & Padula, A. (1996*). Sex and revolution: Women in socialist Cuba.* Oxford University Press.

Smith, L., & Padula, A. (1998). *Sex and revolution: Woman in Socialist Cuba.* Oxford University Press.

Worrall, S. (2016, October 28). When the mob owned Cuba. *Smithsonian Magazine.* https://www.smithsonianmag.com/travel/mob-havana-cuba-culture-music-book-tj-english-cultural-travel-180960610/

CHAPTER 6

PRIVILEGE

As has been mentioned in previous chapters, I was surprised NOT to hear from most of my interviewees about the benefits the exiles had as immigrants. I was unaware of these privileges until I began my research but upon reading about them, it is clear that Lilia, Jack, and the other exiles and their families benefitted significantly from policies and practices that no other immigrant group at the time, nor since, has been afforded. Ester was the only one to comment on privilege, which she did briefly in our interview but also in her writing previously. Enrique noted that there were some help services but implied that the family did not utilize them. It is unclear to what degree they did, but they obviously did in some fashion. Similarly, Lilia only mentioned HIAS as a source of assistance when they first moved. No one mentioned the immigration policies, the federal, state, and local assistance, nor even the privileges they had and still have as a family.

Privilege is not my word choice; rather it is drawn from literature. Eckstein (2022) to the advantages Cubans received as "Cuban privilege." That term that did not go well with the Cuban community in Miami when her book Cuban privilege: The making of immigrant inequality in America was released. Newly elected Miami-Dade County Commissioner Kevin Cabrera, who had not yet taken office nor read the book or any of Eckstein's other work on the island, tweeted angrily after FIU's Cuban Research Institute (CRI) agreed to host a book talk by

Shiksa Speaks: A White, Non-Jew's Understanding of the
Cuban Jewish Diaspora and Its Legacy, 97–108.
Copyright © 2025 *Laura Finley*
Published under exclusive licence by Emerald Publishing Limited
HB: 978-1-83708-494-4, PB: 978-1-83708-495-1, ePDF: 978-1-83708-496-8

Eckstein. "It is shocking that @FIU's Cuban Research Institute would welcome such hate-filled, inflammatory, anti-Cuban rhetoric to Miami-Dade County, home to the largest Cuban diaspora and the global capital of Cuban American exiles." Right-wing Spanish radio and others denounced FIU for hosting Eckstein, which actually increased demand for tickets to the talk. CRI Director Jorge Duany attempted to appease the outraged Cuban Americans and pundits, even inviting human rights activist Orlando Gutiérrez-Boronat to share the stage as a discussant. Approximately 20 Trump supporters stood outside the venue heckling attendees. Inside the tense atmosphere, Eckstein spent the first fifteen minutes outlining the central tenets of her book then turned things over to Gutiérrez-Boronat. Rather than addressing her points about immigration policies that have favored Cubans, Gutiérrez-Boronat reiterated the abuses of the Castro regime and of Cuba today and tried to discredit Eckstein's social science. Duany did not give her a chance to rebut his critique, instead opening the floor to questions and comments (Contreras, 2022).

But through careful historical review, it is clear that privilege is indeed the appropriate term. Starting with President Eisenhower and through eleven different presidencies, policies have been put in place that make it easier for Cubans and their families to come to the US, to obtain legal permanent residency status, to become naturalized citizens, and to bring over family members (Eckstein, 2022). Padgett (2022) commented about the controversy over Eckstein's speech: "To wit: In order to challenge the thesis that the Cuban community has received privileges, said community is asserting its privileges." Like Eckstein (2022), I have no intent of critiquing the people who took advantage of policies and programs offered to them. Rather, the point is to acknowledge the privilege, understand how it shaped Cubans' immigrant experience in different ways, while also applauding what Cubans, and these Jewbans in particular, did with those advantages.

CUBAN PRIVILEGE IN IMMIGRATION POLICY

Some privileges to Cubans were in place even before the revolution. Eckstein (2022) explained that during the Batista era, the United States issued tourist visas to middle- and upper-class Cubans who vacationed and shopped in the US. By the end of 1960, the Eisenhower administration was issuing 1,600 tourist visas to Cubans each week, which it did in a far more expedited fashion than is typical of the process. "The Eisenhower administration understood that the Cubans to whom it issued visas were not typical tourists. Nonetheless, tourist visas provided a basis for admission." Once those tourist visas expired, the US gave the Cubans "involuntary indefinite departure" or "extended voluntary departure," sparing them from the risk of deportation because if they were deported they would have to wait ten years before attempting to reenter the US (Eckstein, 2022). The initial idea behind privileging Cuban immigrants with visa waivers was to help evacuate US agents and their families and was supposed to last only a limited time. These individuals, generally Batista supporters, were often leery of denouncing the Castro regime too vigorously and feared that they would be targeted for retaliation due to the advantages they received. Yet it has lasted decades. For some time, Cubans were even privileged at the expense of other immigrants, as they received essentially first dibs among quotas set for Western Hemisphere immigrants. Congress even gave Cubans their own quota, independent from other immigrants in the region, via an amendment to the Immigration and Nationality Act in 1976. Further, until recent times, even Cuban immigrants who were unauthorized were accepted and given many of the same privileges. Eckstein commented, "Most immigrants from Cuba have arrived without authorization, they come without visas," she says. "But Cubans have been able to come by any means—in a boat, by land, as tourists, whatever—and then have been able to have their status adjusted, so they are lawful immigrants with a path to citizenship" (in Brown, 2022). This is in stark contrast to other immigrant groups, for example, Haitians, who were largely detained and deported if they attempted to enter the US unauthorized. Eckstein (2022) is critical of the disparate treatment of other desperate groups like Haitians. In 1960, President Eisenhower created a presidential commission on Cuban "refugees" and allocated funds for it. President John F. Kennedy continued and expanded the program, calling it the Cuban Refugee Assistance Program (CRA). Kennedy authorized $4 million for the program in fiscal year 1960–1961. In creating the CRA, Kennedy directed Secretary of Health, Education and Welfare Abraham Ribikoff to:

> 1. Provide all possible assistance to voluntary relief agencies in providing necessities for many of the refugees, for resettling as many of them as possible, and for securing jobs for them. 2. Obtain the assistance of both private and governmental agencies to provide useful employment opportunities for displaced Cubans, consistent with the overall employment situation prevailing in Florida. 3. Provide supplemental funds for the resettlement of refugees in other areas, including transportation and adjustment costs to the new communities and for their eventual return to Miami for repatriation to their homeland as soon as that is again possible. 4. Furnish financial assistance to meet, basic maintenance requirements of needy Cuban refugee families in the Miami area as required in communities of resettlement, administered through Federal, State, and local channels, and based on standards used in the community involved. 5. Provide for essential health services through the financial assistance program supplemented by child health, public health services, and other arrangements as needed. 6. Furnish Federal assistance for local public school operating costs related to the unforeseen impact of Cuban refugee children on local teaching facilities. 7. Initiate needed measures to augment training and educational opportunities for Cuban refugees, including physicians, teachers, and those with other professional backgrounds. 8. Provide financial aid for the care and protection of unaccompanied children-the most defenseless and troubled group among the refugee population. 9. Undertake a surplus food distribution program to be administered by the county welfare department, with surplus foods distributed by public and voluntary agencies to needy refugees. (Mitchell, 1962, pp. 3–4).

In sum, Cuban immigrants were able to receive comprehensive and significant public benefits, including food assistance, job training, language instruction, help finding housing and more. Powell (2022) reported that 70 percent of the exiles registered for help with the Cuban Refugee Emergency Center, which they called El Refugio. Although information is scarce, there were also low-cost Cuban loans that could be used for college education (Powell, 2022, p. 5) described another benefit of the program, noting that help was provided in cash (coordinated by the Florida Department of Public Welfare) and "in such a manner as to preserve the dignity and pride of the recipients. The levels of help are in keeping with those provided United States nationals in similar circumstances." It included coverage for hospitalization for acute problems and obstetric needs, immunizations, and child welfare exams, as well as the provision of surplus agricultural commodities. Through the program, Miami Dade schools received assistance to provide education and summer day camps for Cuban children. Further, the federal government reimbursed Miami Dade schools for fifty percent of the cost per Cuban pupil. The school district also received funds to provide English instruction for adults. In December 1960, a Refugee Emergency Center was established in Miami to coordinate assistance as well. Resettlement efforts covered virtually the entire cost of resettling, including transportation and incidental expenses. Help was also provided by nonprofit organizations that received financial assistance from the CRA. These included the National Catholic Welfare Conference, the Church World Service, the United Hebrew Immigrant Aid Society, and the International Rescue Committee (Mitchell, 1962). Simultaneously, an information campaign was launched to promote the fact that Miami was now home to many people who were educated and skilled in hopes of finding the immigrants jobs. Cubans could get loans of up to one thousand per academic year, with larger amounts available for graduate school and professional programs, which covered at least one third and in some cases all of the cost of higher education (Powell, 2022). Many Cuban doctors who immigrated could not practice medicine because they lacked US medical licensure, so some colleges began offering courses to help Cuban doctors pass state licensing exams. Private companies, including Eli Lilly and Upjohn gave money to support a medical training program (Eckstein, 2022).

Mitchell (1962) noted that not all Cuban migrants accepted these services and many who did struggle with it. "The Cuban refugees are, on the whole, men and women who in their own country had never needed or received assistance. Having to accept aid is one of the hardships they have reluctantly assumed as "exiles for conscience's sake." Those who have left Cuba since December of 1960 could bring with them their clothing but little else. They could and can bring no furniture and only five depreciated pesos-worth perhaps 50 cents" (p. 7).

Why did the government bend over backward to assist Cubans at this time and not to other groups? Eckstein (2022) explains that "President Eisenhower, the first to privilege Cubans, did so to leverage immigration for foreign policy geopolitical gain. He set a precedent that subsequent presidents, and Congress, elaborated on, even after it became apparent that the privileging of Cubans did not accomplish the foreign policy goal for which it was intended, and, arguably, strengthened Castros' hold on power by ridding Cuba of regime opponents" (p. 331). That is, various administrations thought they would destabilize the Castro regime but instead, it resulted in a mass exodus of most of the people who had political, social, and financial power to topple it. She commented in an interview, "Without the Cold War, I don't think the Cubans would have gotten these benefits," Eckstein says. The US government was "concerned about quote-unquote communism in our backyard. I think they were more concerned about Cuba than they would have been about a comparable revolution anyplace else in the world" (Brown, 2022).

When in late 1961 the Castro administration started requiring Cubans to fund their travel in hard currency, which many did not have. Never mind, the Kennedy administration pitched in $350,000 to transport Cubans to the United States and even requested that Congress set aside $10 million annually to do so (Eckstein, 2022). Between 1959 and 1962, some 1,600–1,700 Cubans arrived on commercial flights each week. Further, between December 1960 and October 1962, the US sponsored the travel of more than 14,000 unaccompanied minors of Operation Pedro Pan, of which Marcos was one. This was a program, administrated by the CIA, interestingly, that was concocted to help get the children of Cuban underground members out of the country. It ended up including many others, however, with a cost to taxpayers of $28,500,000 (Eckstein, 2022). Until the US broke diplomatic relations with Cuba on January 3, 1961, Cubans could easily get regular visas at the US embassy in Havana or at the consulate in Santiago. After that, the US began extending visa waivers (Eckstein, 2022).

In 1965 when Castro lifted exit restrictions and some five thousand Cubans left from Camarioca (discussed in more detail in Chapter 7), the Johnson administration paroled the new arrivals and offered them emergency assistance. Unlike any other immigrant group, the Coast Guard was even authorized to help them make it ashore if their boats were having trouble (Eckstein, 2022). Extending further the benefits, the Johnson administration helped many Cuban immigrants in the mid-1960s be transported to the United States at taxpayer expense, through Freedom Flights. These ran between December 1, 1965, and April 6, 1973, transporting more than 250,000 Cubans to Miami. Flights ran twice daily, five days per week. Nearly a third of a million Cubans, "most of whose lives were not at risk," were transported to the US in this way during the Kennedy, Johnson, and Nixon administrations (Eckstein, 2022). Those flights cost the US more than $4,000,000 (Time, 1971). The Freedom Flights were "the largest and longest refugee resettlement initiative in U.S (Duany, 2017). Along with the transportation, the Johnson administration also authorized $12,600,00 in funds to help the new Cubans acclimate, all at the same time as immigration law was ending country-based admissions (Eckstein, 2022).

Another privilege afforded to Cubans but not given to many other groups who would seemingly be as, if not more, deserving, is the social construction of refugee status (Eckstein, 2022). Cubans have at times been considered refugees, despite not having to show that they were particularly fleeing persecution. As noted, once their tourist visas expired, the first exiles were reimagined into different statuses, including refugee, which meant they could not be forced to return to Cuba. As Eckstein noted, "the only criteria that Cubans needed to get access to this generous program was to have come to the United States after January 1959.… This was a way of getting around immigration law" (in Brown, 2022). "If the United States only reluctantly and belatedly admitted Jewish refugees who fled persecution during World War II, the Eisenhower administration was quick to imagine Cubans as refugees, even when their lifestyle but not lives were at risk" (Eckstein, 2022, p. 9). Eckstein (2022) explained, "Most Cubans received benefits as 'imagined refugees,' that is, as persons who successive administrations defined as refugees so that they could qualify for entitlements for which they otherwise could not, and who, as imagined, qualified for more benefits even than 'real refugees,' that is, persons who fled persecution or likely persecution, the near-universally agreed definition of refugees" (p. 43). Even at times when official policy determined Cubans not to be refugees, they were de facto treated as such. "Cubans benefitted from being considered refugees, both real and imagined. Doors accordingly were opened to them that were closed to other nationals, including to persons who were more deserving of admission as refugees and more deserving of refugee benefits" (p. 334). Those Cubans who immigrated when Castro came to power were considered refugees automatically. The designation of refugee for these initial immigrants fleeing the island post-revolution came upon entry to the US. All other groups of refugees were screened and vetted abroad before entering the US. This even included persons who had left Cuba and were safely settled in other countries, despite US law specifying that such individuals did not qualify as refugees. Eckstein (2022) referred to these benefits as the "most expansive set of federal government-funded refugee benefits in US history" (p. 319). Today, per the Refugee Act of 1980, to qualify as a refugee one must not be able to return to their home country due to "persecution or a well-founded fear of persecution on account of race, religion, nationality, membership in a particular social group, or political opinion." Further, the Department of Homeland Security only gives someone refugee status after rigorous screening and interviews (Powell, 2022, p. 255). In 1961 a Miami-Dade County Commissioner questioned before Congress whether the Cuban immigrants were truly refugees (Eckstein, 2022). In 1966, the Johnson administration even extended the meaning of "being Cuban" to relatives of Cubans living in the United States but resided in third countries. They were not required to have been born in Cuba or ever lived there (Eckstein, 2022).

Cuban exiles could also get bank loans from the Small Business Administration (SBA) that were far more generous than for other groups. Powell (2022) reported that between 1968 and 1980, 46 percent of SBA loans went to Cubans. No one in this family had any knowledge of the exiles receiving loans but it seems likely that they must have, given that they started businesses and came to the US with little capital.

The privileges afforded to Cubans had a positive payoff, as Cubans thrived in places like Miami and have helped turn it into a dynamic city. With the benefit of lawful permanent status and the generous benefits, including in education and training, many Cuban immigrants were now qualified for professional jobs that propelled them to economic success. As Eckstein (2022) noted, "it did not take long for Cuban immigrants to make impressive economic gains. Many of them earned more than they had in Cuba, and more than native-born people into whose midst they moved" (p. 60). Cubans in Miami, especially the earlier waves, hold many high-income jobs and influential positions (Eckstein, 2022). Upon settling in and over years and then generations, Cubans became accustomed to their privileges and became

> agents of their own continued privileging. They pressed for more. They came to lobby, make campaign contributions, leverage their vote, and mobilize in the streets of Miami and Washington to defend and promote their interests and concerns on immigration-related, along with other, matters. Settling mainly in Florida, which acquired a mounting number of electoral college votes as more of the country's population settled in the state, they attained outsized political influence, despite comprising less than 1 percent of the total population. In the process, domestic politics replaced foreign policy as the driving force behind Cuban immigrant privileging. (Eckstein, 2022, p. 331)

Over time, the exile Cuban Americans became a powerful voting bloc, owing in large part to the advantage they had to become citizens. By 1980, 60 percent of Cubans across the nation and 51 percent living in Miami were citizens with 56 and 47 percent, respectively, of voting age. They took candidate's stances on Cuba into consideration when voting, supporting candidates that were opposed to Castro or anything they associated with socialism. The Cuban American community elected their own to local, state and eventually national positions. In 1989, Ileana Ros-Lehtinen was the first Cuban immigrant elected to Congress, followed by Lincoln Diaz-Balart and Robert Menendez (Eckstein, 2022). Cuban politicians and the exile voting block (and to a lesser degree, their progeny) have continued to support the US embargo on Cuba, which is, according to Eckstein, no longer necessary. "The embargo doesn't make sense anymore. We have relations with communist China, we have relations with communist Vietnam, and there's no embargo on those countries anymore, and yet we have one on Cuba—why? It's Florida politics, it's the Cuban American lobbyists" (in Brown, 2022).

Since 1966, the Cuban Adjustment Act (CAA) allows Cuban immigrants who had been in the US a fast track to lawful permanent resident status. Sponsored by Senator Edward Kennedy but with widespread bipartisan support, the CAA was signed into law on November 2, 1966. Under the CAA, Cubans can get a Green Card and apply to be lawful residents. Cuban individuals who were admitted or paroled into the US qualified for permanent residence one year and one day after their entry (originally two years) under what was dubbed "humanitarian parole." It helped to regularize the legal situation of the approximately 165,000 Cubans who were living in the states without lawful permanent residence and the result is that virtually all Cubans who came in the early wave were allowed to stay, regardless of how they got here. The CAA also made Cuban immigrants eligible for health and educational benefits through the federal government, while other legal immigrants had to wait five years before they could access those benefits. As Abraham (2015) wrote, "De facto, the CAA turns each and every Cuban reaching the U.S. shore into a meritorious asylee. This is treatment afforded people of absolutely no other nationality" (p. 1). Further, Abraham (20165) explained "The initial theory of the CAA and its advocates was that anyone and everyone fleeing or otherwise leaving Cuba for the ninety-mile trip to the United States was an asylee, that is a victim of "persecution," and one of whom a normal and orderly, documented, and legal exit from Cuba and entry into the United States could not be expected and should not be required. Further, under the CAA, no proof of personal persecution is required. For citizens of all other countries, the fact of arriving in the United States from an "unfree" country is distinctly and definitely not enough to gain asylum and residency. An individual not from Cuba must be able to show that he or she personally is the sought-out, sought-after object of persecution" (pp. 2–3). A year prior to the passage of the CAA, Congress had authorized the Immigration and Nationality Act of 1965 (also known as the Hart-Celler Act). It established a cap on visas for immigrants in the Western Hemisphere, limiting them to 120,000. Correa-Cabrera and Spagat (2020) note that the CAA "did not say anything about whether Cubans would be subject to the new quota system established by the Hart-Celler Act. It simply stated that Cubans could become lawful permanent residents. The problem then was that the U.S. government allocated visa numbers under the Western Hemisphere immigration quota to these Cubans, thereby reducing the visas available to other immigrants from the Western Hemisphere" (p. 1). Eckstein (2022) explained that the CAA did exempt Cubans from the requirement that immigrants from the Western Hemisphere need to apply for lawful permanent residence, which was established with the Hart-Celler Act of 1965. Within a year after the CAA was enacted, some 41,000 Cuban immigrants had their status adjusted and close to 82,500 applied the following year (Eckstein, 2022).

The CAA has become increasingly considered unfair if not racist (Duany, 2017), yet it remains in effect to this day. Eckstein (2022) and Abraham (2015) compare the plight of Cubans with that of Haitians. "Whereas Haitians fleeing their miserable, dangerous, oppressive, and violent island are presumed to be economic migrants, Cubans fleeing their communist island—if not a "communist paradise" certainly a paradise compared to Haiti and many, perhaps most, of the countries of the world—are automatically declared refugees" (Abraham, 2015, p. 3). Gonzalez Maestrey (2022) noted, "The Act legislative history shows that concerns of some members of Congress—regarding the excessive use of parole;

its permanent nature; its contradictions with the migration policy envisaged for Latin America; the impact on employment, fundamentally in black communities; and the possible weakening of the counterrevolutionary mass in Cuba—were outweighed by the more strategic intention of portraying Cuban migration as a testament of the failure of communism, a central component of the US hemispheric foreign policy" (p. 14). Whitney (2022) commented, "The Cuban Adjustment Act (CAA), which concerns Cubans migrating to the United States, receives little attention, while fuss and fury grow over an unprecedented number of migrants, Cubans among them, crossing the U.S. southern border now."

One of the people that Powell (2022) interviewed, expressed in detail the advantages the exiles were given over other immigrant groups and the effect of that today.

> The Cubans were lucky—seems a strange word—but they immigrated during the Cold War. They had everything working: A Democratic Congress. There weren't many immigrants in America at that time, so you didn't have a lot of competition. Plus, these were not typical immigrants. Most immigrants don't come with middle-class values, certainly not the first waves (p. 238).

The same gentleman goes on to comment about massive government assistance programs. He said, "Without a doubt, Cubans acquired most-favored immigrant status. Most people don't talk about that" (Powell, 2022, p. 238).

Some Miami residents, as noted in earlier chapters, were not elated with all the help afforded to Cuban immigrants. Eckstein (2022) explained that some Miamians resented the fact that Cubans who lived in rental units were able to send their children to public schools based on the help the federal government and state had provided but they did not contribute by paying property taxes. "Non-Cuban taxpaying property owners bore the costs, while their children suffered from the crowding of schools caused by the inundation of Cubans" (p. 66). The many privileges afforded to the exile generation of Cubans reinforced to African Americans that the government cared more about Cuban's advancement than about their own. Cuban immigrants received more financial aid monthly than did needy "Negroes," $100 per month compared to $81 per month Only Cubans could get cash assistance immediately while others needing welfare had to reside in Florida for five years. Unemployed Cubans could receive compensation even after their unemployment ran out while unemployed "Negroes" could not. Further, some of the training programs prepared Cubans to do work that "Negroes" had traditionally held, like bellman, porters, elevator operators and chambermen (Eckstein, 2022). The civil rights movement was happening simultaneously, and African Americans saw newcomers being welcomed and supported in ways they were not (Powell, 2022). As Eckstein (2022) wrote, as one president after another extended benefits to Cuban, "at times, Cubans were even privileged *at the expense* of both other foreigners and native-born Americans" (p. xiii) [emphasis original].

NO PRIVILEGE FOR THE CUBAN PEOPLE, THOUGH

Since February 1962, the US has had an economic and trade embargo on Cuba, or blockade, as Cubans call it. The purpose of both was "to weaken and, if possible, topple the communist government of Cuban President Fidel Castro while aiding his victims" (Abraham, 2015, p. 1). Under the embargo, most US companies have been prohibited from dealing with Cuba. Most have considered the embargo to be a terrific failure that has only hurt the Cuban people. President Obama attempted to improve relations with Cuba, reducing restrictions on some businesses and opening up flights between the two countries, but President Trump reversed his strategy and added other measures that also worsened the lives of Cubans. More detail on this is provided in Chapter 7. Both the Cuban government and the United Nations have observed that the embargo has cost the Cuban economy at least $130 billion. The US Chamber of Commerce noted that the embargo has cost the US billions as well. Rhodes (2021) explained, "Sixty years of sanctions have only created hardships for the Cuban people while providing the regime with a convenient scapegoat to blame for all of their country's economic woes and societal discontent." Instead of the embargo, Rhodes (2021) said that the US should build on the Obama administration's efforts to open up travel and commerce. "Exposing Cubans to the freedoms and opportunities available to their American relatives will increase outrage and pressure towards the Cuban government for failing to provide these things. And removing the ability of the Communist Party to blame the United States for its own failures will lay bare the consequences of the Cuban government's unwillingness to shift away from Soviet-era economic policies and political repression." The UN has repeatedly called on the US to end the embargo. Speakers before a hearing on the issue in November 2023 noted the horrible human toll and cited the fact that some 80 percent of Cubans have only known life under the embargo (United Nations, 2023). On November 2, 2023, the UN General Assembly called for the 31st time on the US to end the embargo, a vote that was supported by 186 countries with only the US and Israel voting no (Ukraine abstained). Cuban Foreign Minister Bruno Rodriguez spoke before the assembly, asserting that the "blockade prevents Cuba from accessing food, medicines, and technological and medical equipment" and saying that it "qualifies as a crime of genocide" (Reuters, 2023).

During later waves, the Coast Guard also had a practice, until 1994 of bringing visa-less Cubans to the US when they were repatriating all other groups. Cubans were given temporary entry rights, even allowing them to be admitted as tourists when they were not, thus putting them on the pathway to attain permanent residency status. Further, even those Cubans who did not enter lawfully received full federally funded welfare benefits on arrival, whereas all other unauthorized immigrant groups were ineligible and those who were authorized had to wait five years before they were eligible (Eckstein, 2022).

CONCLUSION

Again, it was interesting to me how little anyone I interviewed seemed to know about the process of leaving Cuba, their admittance into the US, and the services available to them. I imagine had I been able to interview Consuelo, Isaac, Eva, David, or anyone from that generation, I would have heard more about the travels and procedures as they made the arrangements. Jack would likely have remembered more as well, given that he was in his early twenties when they left. I also think part of it, however, is that acknowledging Cuban privilege challenges the "victim of Castro" narrative that has been adopted by this family (and it seems most exiles) and passed down the generations. To admit that there were significant benefits afforded to Cubans would be to imply that they were perhaps not required to be as resilient as is made out. I am in no way denying how emotionally traumatic it must have been to leave one's home country amidst chaos and uncertainty. But, as Eckstein (2009, 2022) and others have shown, many other immigrants before and after from different countries have done so but without such support. She suggests that rather than remove the benefits Cubans have and continue to receive, the US should consider affording them to other groups. Pointing to the success of the exile generation, Eckstein maintains that doing so would help other immigrant groups to experience similar financial stability and easier integration. After reading and learning a bit more about immigration policy (I admit, I have a LOT more to learn!), I concur.

REFERENCES

Abraham, D. (2015, May). The Cuban Adjustment Act of 1966: Past and future. *Research Solutions.* https://media.law.miami.edu/faculty-administration/pdf/david-abraham/cuban-adj-act.pdf

Brown, J. (2022, August 1). *Why is the Cuban immigrant story in the US so different from others?* BU Today. https://www.bu.edu/articles/2022/cuban-immigrant-story-in-us-is-different-from-others/

Contreras, J. (2022, December 29). Miami's fight over Cuban privilege. *Washington Monthly.* https://washingtonmonthly.com/2022/12/29/miamis-fight-over-cuban-privilege/

Correa-Cabrera, G., & Spagat, E. (2020,October). *U.S. immigration policy for Cubans: From revolution to COVID-19.* Wilson Center. https://www.wilsoncenter.org/sites/default/files/media/uploads/documents/FINAL%20U.S.%20IMMIGRATION%20POLICY%20FOR%20CUBANS-%20FROM%20REVOLUTION%20TO%20CO-VID-19_0.pdf

Duany, J. (2017, July 6). *Cuban migration: A post revolution exodus ebbs and flows.* Migration Policy Institute. https://www.migrationpolicy.org/article/cuban-migration-postrevolution-exodus-ebbs-and-flows

Eckstein, S. (2009). *The immigrant divide: How Cubans changes the US and their homeland.* Routledge.

Eckstein, S. (2022). *Cuban privilege: The making of immigrant inequality in America.* Cambridge University Press.

Gonzalez Maestrey, R. (2022). Attempts to repeal the Cuban Adjustment Act. *International Journal of Cuban Studies, 14*(1), 13–35.

Mitchell, W. (1962, March). *The Cuban Refugee Program.* https://www.ssa.gov/policy/docs/ssb/v25n3/v25n3p3.pdf

Padgett, T. (2022, December 8). *Cubans challenge the claim that they're privileged... by asserting their privilege.* WLRN. https://www.wlrn.org/commentary/2022-12-08/cubans-challenge-the-claim-that-theyre-privileged-by-asserting-their-privilege

Powell, D. (2022). *Ninety miles and a lifetime away: Memories of early Cuban exiles.* University of Florida Press

Rhodes, C. (2021, July 21). *The US embargo on Cuba has failed.* Al Jazeera. https://www.aljazeera.com/opinions/2021/7/21/the-us-embargo-on-cuba-has-failed

Powell, D. (2023). *Ninety miles and a lifetime away: Memories of early Cuban exiles.* University Press of Florida.

Reuters. (2023, November 2). *U.N. votes to end US embargo on Cuba; U.S. and Israel oppose.* https://www.reuters.com/world/americas/un-votes-end-us-embargo-cuba-us-israel-oppose-2023-11-02/

Time. (1971, September 13). CUBA: End of the freedom flights. https://content.time.com/time/subscriber/article/0,33009,903113,00.html

United Nations. (2023, November 1). *Economic, commercial embargo imposed by United States against Cuba, harmful, violates UN charter, speakers underline in General Assembly.* https://press.un.org/en/2023/ga12552.doc.htm

Whitney, W. (2022, October 18). *The Cuban Adjustment Act still privileges Cuban migrants to the U.S. but hurts Cuba.* People's World. https://www.peoplesworld.org/article/the-cuban-adjustment-act-still-privileges-cuban-migrants-to-the-u-s-but-hurts-cuba/

CHAPTER 7

CUBA POST-EXILE, MEH

Given how everyone in this family loves to tell people about their Cuban history, I was shocked to find that almost no one had any interest in knowing what is going on in Cuba or in supporting Cuban people. For instance, no on mentioned US policy toward Cuba, including its continued sanctions. All but Ester and David seemed to believe that anything anti-Communist is good, even if not for the Cuban people. For example, when asked how he felt about the Castros and the current leadership and political situation in Cuba, Perry answered "It's awful and sad. I remember growing up he was always pained as a villain. I sometimes wonder what life would have been like without him coming in power and my parents staying in Cuba and growing up there, kinda weird. It is such a shame that the world has allowed the Castros to come in and allowed a country to be decimated."

> Even Ester admitted that she once shared these thoughts, although has since been more reflective on her family, her identity, and Cuba. "As a young person I had accepted the Miami Cubans community's official political line, incorporating it into my own passionately held vision of emancipation from my family: I would never choose to live in a country which interfered with my precious freedom to speak my mind. Unspoken though not forgotten were my early childhood memories of hearing my family, like many others, speak of Fidel Castro as a hero who would restore Cuba's proud heritage as a nation committed to social justice" (Rok, 1995, p. 91).

Shiksa Speaks: A White, Non-Jew's Understanding of the
Cuban Jewish Diaspora and Its Legacy, 109–122.
Copyright © 2025 *Laura Finley*
Published under exclusive licence by Emerald Publishing Limited
HB: 978-1-83708-494-4, PB: 978-1-83708-495-1, ePDF: 978-1-83708-496-8

It is possible that these individuals are not really aware of the details of the continued embargo and the US listing of Cuba on the terrorist watch list. No one discussed the subsequent waves of Cuban immigrants, the tremendously difficult migration they endured, nor how they were received. Not a single interviewee mentioned offering assistance to the later Cuban migrants. There was also no mention of exiles involved in assassination attempts in Cuba or in violence in Miami, nor of the controversial handling by the US of Elian Gonzalez. I was also surprised to learn that despite nostalgia for their Jewish life in Cuba, it does not seem that anyone in the family donates to support the Patronato, which is in desperate need of help.

Only two of the persons I interviewed, my husband David and his mom's cousin Ester, the professor, expressed any interest in Cuba today nor any real knowledge of what has gone on there since the revolution. In fact, most expressed that they do not want to know. Perhaps this is because their entire families left, so they are not in a position to have to worry about family on the island. Likewise, all of their friends left, so they really seem to have put Cuba into the past. If they say anything about it, most of these interviewees say negative things about communism, poverty, and crime. I guess I should not have been surprised, as prior research showed that most exiles never went back to Cuba, and many were very judgmental of those who did, even the New Cubans who largely still had family on the island. Of those who did return, exiles still tended to filter their experience through their anti-Castro eyes, viewing the island as far less magnificent than in their youthful memories. Jewbans who returned did attempt to rebuild synagogues and other Jewish sites, but the numbers remain small (Eckstein, 2009). As Behar (1995) wrote,

> Cuba since the revolution has been imagined as either a utopia of a backward police state. Cuba, viewed with utopian eyes, is a defiant little island that has dared to step on the toes of a great superpower and dreamed ambitiously of undoing the legacy of poverty, inequality, and unfulfilled revolutions that has plagued Latin America and the Caribbean. Alternately, as newspaper headlines in the U.S. media like to declare, Cuba is 'an island of lost souls,' a place where 'huddled masses yearn for the comforts of life' and will sacrifice everything to leave, plunging into the 'deadly sea of dreams' as *balseros* (raft people)or Cuban 'wetbacks.' Within this conflicting web or representations born of the Cold War, there is little room for a more nuances and complex vision of how Cubans on the island and in the diaspora give meaning to their lives, their identity, and their culture in the aftermath of a battle that has split the nation at the root (p. 2).

Similarly, Risech (1995) wrote about his realization that there might be more than just two perspectives on Cuba.

> As I grew older the gap between the Anglocentric environment of school and the world of arroz con pollo, dominos and the music of Lecuona grew increasingly difficult to negotiate, but in the end it was politics that made it unbridgeable. Initially,

I had only the knowledge of Cuba that I had received from my family, and it only slowly dawned on me that there were other perspectives to account for. I date my major political break with my family, and by extension with Cuban Miami, to May 1970: once I knew it was possible for my relatives to approve of the massacre of unarmed students at Kent State ('for less communists,' they said), I began to question all of their positions, including those on Cuba. It was not long before I had read enough to realize that they knew very little about the real Cuba, the post-1959 Cuba that they had fled en masse. The more I read, the more alien I felt in Miami, as I found that even though I had reservations about their policies, I did not hate but rather admired Fidel and Che Guevara for their courage in the face of implacable U.S. aggression and for their efforts to improve living standards for most Cubans. The very fact that I read the things that I did set me apart from Cuban Miami in ways I did not fully grasp at the time. Though I still felt in certain profound ways at home in Cuban Miami, in others I knew I was no more one of *them* than someone from another planet (pp. 61–62).

As Behar explained, the people I interviewed are not entirely wrong, but they are not totally correct, either. Instead, Cuba remains a country that is struggling economically, but crime is quite low. The people are amazingly friendly and resilient. Having been fortunate enough to spend several days in Cuba learning from several tour guides and residents of Havana, Cubans today will admit that communism has been both good and bad to them. They applaud the free education and universal healthcare but explain that daily life is difficult, as many things we take for granted are scarce on the island. The people we met, however, were still proud to be Cuban and were very enthusiastic about sharing a drink, a dance, and a story.

On our trip we were fortunate to take an amazing day tour of Jewish Havana in a 1959 Chevy Impala with a fantastic bilingual tour guide, Ronald. He told us that he went to college and trained to be a teacher but was dismayed when he worked in Cuban schools as an English and Social Studies teacher that the curriculum was super prescriptive and the methods not at all what he had learned about engaging students. He also noted that he made a lot more money as a freelance tour guide than as an educator but appreciated that he was still able to share things that he knew with his clients. We had a detailed conversation about how some places in the US are moving in this same direction. As a resident of Florida, I have witnessed Governor Ron DeSantis spearhead efforts to narrow curricula, to weaken conversations about critical issues like race, gender, sexual orientation, and gender identity, and to ban books, among other concerning changes.

Our tour guides took us to the Patronato, where we met the man who continues to run it. He was a lovely human who struggles to not only provide Jewish cultural and religious services but also to assist as many people in need as possible. He expressed that they rely heavily on donors, as the Cuban currency is essentially worthless.

In this chapter, I provide a brief review of the post-exile waves of Cuban immigrants to the US and discuss their reception. The chapter also critiques US policy on Cuba since the 1970s, despite my interviewees lack of interest in these issues.

CUBAN MIGRATION POST-EXILE

First, it is important to recognize that while the exiles left Cuba via airplane, many who wanted to leave could not afford airfare, lacked passports, or could not obtain visas. Some left in small, unsafe boats, trying to reach Florida. After the Cuban Missile Crisis in October 1962, commercial travel between the US and Cuba was suspended. This led to a rise in clandestine, dangerous travel, much of it by small inner tubes and makeshift vessels. Between 1962 and 1965, approximately 6,700 "boat people," or *balseros*, arrived in Florida. By June 1, 1965, the US Coast Guard had assisted 6,862 Cubans making the trek over sea. 1965 was the first of three times the Cuban government allowed people to leave for the US without US authorization—from Camarioca in 1965, Mariel in 1980, and the *balsero* crises in 1994. Most experts argue another exodus began in 2021 and persists as of this writing. Each of these waves has brought Cubans who are more reflective of the island—darker skin, working class, and often in desperate poverty (American Experience 2005)

In the mid and later 1960s, discontent with the Castro regime was widespread, and it was coupled by economic hardships. Castro closed down 55,000 small businesses in 1968 and virtually eliminated private property. An increasing number of Cubans turned against the revolution. Amidst mounting pressure, Castro opened the port of Camarioca, allowing people who wanted to go to "the Yankee Paradise" to leave and for relatives from Miami to come collect their loved ones. It was open from October 10, 1965, to November 15, 1965. Almost 3,000 Cubans took advantage. In order to leave, Cubans had to forfeit any land or property and apply with the Ministry of Interior. The Freedom Flights described in Chapter 2 also brought Cubans to the Miami, with some 250,000 Cubans arriving in the US by 1974 (U.S. Department of Defense, 2020).

More Cubans continued to flee to the US in the 1970s, and while not an amazing relationship, tensions between the two countries had lessened somewhat. After a series of *Dialogos* (dialogues) in 1978 between Cuban officials and exiles in the US, a travel policy was established that allowed some 100,000 exiles living in the US to visit Cuba. To my knowledge, no one in this family took advantage of that. A consequence of this was an increase in the number of people seeking to leave Cuba. In April 1980 a surge of 10,000 Cubans stormed the Peruvian embassy in Cuba seeking permission to leave, Castro responded by opening the Port of Mariel, much like he had done in Camarioca. Between April and October 1980, some 125,000 Cubans left Mariel. They became known as the *Marielitos*. They arrived in Key West, having survived the trip on crowded ships. Any people with relatives already in the US were processed first, while those without relatives were housed in tent cities in Miami Dade County, where they lived for several months (Stephens, 2021).

The *Marielitos* were not well-received by Cubans or much of anyone living in South Florida. Although they were first referred to as the "Freedom Flotilla," things quickly changed. There was widespread speculation that Castro had opened the doors largely to prisoners and other "undesirables" who were "invading" the

US, although this turned out to be false. In reality, only four percent had criminal records and many of those were as political prisoners. Nonetheless, media circulated rumors and movies like Scarface (1983) reinforced the stereotype. Negative stereotypes in Cuba and the US about the alleged criminality of darker-skinned people made these rumors all too easy to believe, as many of the *Marielitos* were Black or of mixed race. Few bothered to question its truth or look into the diverse reasons the *Marielitos* had for leaving Cuba (Stephens, 2021).

One clear sign of the negative reception of the *Marielitos* was on May 6, 1981, when Democratic Governor of Florida Bob Graham testified before a joint hearing of the House and Senate subcommittees on immigrations, stating, "We cannot subsidize fail[e]d foreign societies and their undesirables with a policy that declares in effect anyone who can land their feet on the sands of Florida's beaches has permanent license to run through Florida's streets. Since the Federal Government was unwilling to enforce the immigration laws when illegal criminal aliens entered our country last summer, it must take responsibility for expelling those individuals now." Graham was clear that his comments were about the *Marielitos* and was insistent that the burden of receiving the *Marielitos* would be crippling to South Florida communities (Stephens, 2021).

Another rumor about the *Marielitos* was that many were homosexual. Wildly exaggerated, there were some people who were homosexual on the boats, and they feared that they would be harassed as they had in Cuba (see Chapter 5). And, unlike earlier waves and in particular the exiles, a disproportionate number of the *Marielitos* were single men who on the whole do not elicit much humanitarian sympathy (Stephens, 2021).

One more difference is that few *Marielitos* benefitted from the same type of resources that welcomed the exiles. The Refugee Act of 1980, which was approved by Congress just one month before the start of the boatlift, changed the criteria for refugee asylum and added legal maneuverings for Cubans to be paroled. The executive branch could now parole large groups coming into the US and exceed the refugee cap of 50,000 only in cases of "an unforeseen emergency refugee situation" prompted by "grave humanitarian concerns" or "the national interest." President Carter reportedly did not exercise this provision because of political pressure not to "reward illegal entry" or "set a dangerous precedent" that might shape admission of other groups trying to unlawfully enter the US. Instead, it paroled the *Marielitos* and gave them a special temporary status, which had to be renewed by Congress in six months. This meant they could not qualify for refugee benefits like those received by the exiles. Eventually, most *Marielitos* did qualify for federal assistance, but they received nowhere near the degree of help as the previous waves and their status was always tenuous rather than certain. Many faced scrutiny by neighbors and police, who continued to cast them as would-be criminals. This occurred at a time when conservative politicians and pundits began to whip up frenzy about illegal immigration. Eventually many of the exiles rejected them. They did so because they bought into the criminal myth, in part. Also,

A community that had cultivated an identity closely associated with assimilation and economic success started to perceive the new arrivals as potential threats. Racial thinking decisively shaped this process.21 An estimated 95 percent of the Cubans who entered the U.S. between 1959 and 1979 identified as White. While they initially encountered discrimination, most benefited from their proximity to Whiteness as it functioned in the United States. Yet their place within the country's racial order was "conditional" in ways that made many Cubans sensitive to changes that might undermine their collective position (Stephens, 2021).

Due to the earlier waves being largely White, the practice of first resettling those who had family in the US again provided racial privilege. Those without connections were sent to resettlement camps around the country. In these camps, darker-skinned Cubans had a harder time getting out, as they had to find a "sponsor" who would agree to help them find work and a place to live. Many people were unwilling to host Black or mulato Cubans in their homes. Housing in Miami was difficult to find any way, as the rental rate vacancy at the time was less than one percent. Some were housed in temporary "tent city" in what is now the home stadium of the Miami Dolphins. More negative media considered these men to be freeloaders, seeing them as able-bodied yet unwilling to work (Stephens, 2021). After tent city, many ended up on the streets. Police began arresting people for trespassing and sleeping outside, and local officials continued to call for federal assistance. And, as Stephens (2021) noted, Almost all the Cubans already established in Miami, moreover, had benefited from a uniquely favorable set of immigration policies. This left few organized groups prepared to recognize the particular challenges facing Black and *mulato* Mariel Cubans who, like Haitians, lacked refugee status."

Another exodus from Cuba came in the summer of 1994. When the Soviet Union collapsed in 1989, Cuba lost its primary supplier of goods and the economy had tanked. It shrunk some 40 percent in three years. Starting in May of 1994, 33,000 Cubans fled the island, either on boats they hijacked or those they were able to construct out of anything and everything. This group became known as *Balseros* (rafters).Initially, President Bill Clinton responded harshly, authorizing the U.S. Coast Guard to intercept them in the Straits of Florda and take them to the US military base in Guantanamo Bay, Cuba. Approximately 35,000 *Balseros* attempted to leave Cuba, with many picked up by the Coast Guard. Clinton reversed course outrage amid outrage and political pressure by exiles, and the *Balseros* were released from Guantanamo Bay in 1995 (American Experience, 2005). These later waves resulted in ten percent of revolutionary Cuba's population leaving the island and drove a wedge in the Cuban American community in South Florida. Powell (2022) noted, "In one view, the early refugees shunned the newcomers and thus impeded them in their efforts to succeed; moreover, the newcomers had lower levels of education and fewer marketable skills" (p. 226–227). The new migrants also had a different view of Cuba than the nostalgic one of the exiles, largely because they weren't even alive before the revolution.

2022 and 2023, saw huge new waves of Cuban migrants flooding into South Florida. According to the Coast Guard and US Customs and Border Protection, five times more migrants arrived in South Florida in 2022 than the year prior. In just two days in November 2022, more than 180 Cubans were taken into custody as they tried to enter the Florida Keys. Although not all from Cuba, between October 1 and December 14, more than 2,350 migrants were taken into federal custody in South Florida and another almost 3,000 migrants were detained at sea by the Coast Guard. Monroe County (home to the Florida Keys) has been particularly hard hit, and it is overwhelming local resources. Monroe County Sheriff Rick Ramsay stated, "The mass migration is depleting critical staff from doing their assigned duties of protecting, responding, investigating and patrolling our communities." Because immigration is dealt with largely by federal authorities, Ramsay and his patrolmen are largely powerless to do much more than wait for U.S Border Patrol agents to arrive. He said that migrant calls are flooding 911, and that such calls typically necessitate contacting several agencies, including the U.S Coast Guard, Florida Fish and Wildlife Conservation Commission, fire rescue, healthcare services and more. Ramsay cited an approximately 600 percent increase in migration to the Keys and chastises the federal government for providing few resources. Many are arriving on dilapidated boats that are leaking pollutants, damaging the waterways (Goodhue, 2023).

Unlike the exiles or the previous Cuban migrants, these new Cuban immigrants are not always greenlighted to stay in the US. Filosa (2022) reported that the United States Coast Guard today does return Cubans migrants to the island, and on December 10, 2022—just one day—two Coast Guard crews returned 152 Cubans to their home country. During the first weekend of January 2023, the Coast Guard responded to more than 500 Cuban migrants reaching the Keys. Cuba's leader, Miguel Díaz-Canel acknowledged that 2022 was "one of the most challenging of Cuba's revolutionary history" and that 2023 was likely to be even worse. It seems as though it was. One person who took the dangerous trek across the water, 36-year-old Jeiler del Toro Diaz, said "I would prefer to die to reach my dream and help my family. The situation in Cuba is not very good." He and the others who came with him took three months to plan their trip and to build their boat from metal boards, 55-gallon tanks, and tree nails. He had to sell his house in order to help fund the trip. At one point their boat broke down and none of the cruise ships or the plane flying by offered assistance, so they threw their batteries, fuel, and cargo overboard and starting rowing. When they saw the first signs of land they swam and waded through mud until reaching the coast. Miami immigration lawyer Willy Allen explained that many more Cuban migrants should be expected, noting "the desperation that exists among Cubans to leave, who have no hope that the economy or the Cuban government will improve in a way that helps them." Cubans today have to stand in long lines to get money from banks, to get gas, and to get most consumer goods. Many other Cubans are reaching the US-Mexico border. A total of nearly 225,000 Cubans arrived in the US in 2022, which makes it one of the highest years since Castro took power in 1959. One migrant remained hopeful that this wave will finally bring significant change to Cuba. Armando Sardinas, who had been imprisoned for participating in anti-government protests in 2021, explained, "The current exodus will lead the Cuban government to accept its failure as a government and of its communist ideology, and there will be a change. The people are already desperate; many fear for their future here in Cuba if the current government continues to rule this country" (Goodhue, 2023).

Another cause for concern among Cubans is Diaz-Canel's leadership. One Cuba expert, Sebastian Arcos from Florida International University' (FIU) Cuban Research Institute, said, "He has no charisma, and the population simply perceives him as a person who is incompetent, who is weak and who is also a puppet of others, specifically Raúl Castro. Without political legitimacy, there is no hope for the population. There is no chance that people will believe that the government is capable of fixing anything" (Torres & Ortiz-Blanes, 2023). As is clear, Cuba continues to struggle economically. Many people survive by *inventor*, or hustling, similar to what our tour guide Ronald explained. The coronavirus exacerbated problems and the embargo as well as listing as a State Sponsor of Terror continued to make distribution of humanitarian aid difficult. Fall 2023 saw rolling blackouts that only worsened the scarcity of fuel, food, and medicines. Restrictions on power usage were issued by many local governments. Some blackouts lasted eight to ten hours per day in areas outside of the capital. Cuba has relied on oil from Venezuela but corruption and chaos in that country has slowed the imports. These conditions have led to many demonstrations both in Cuba and in the US (Reuters in Havana, 2023). While this is prompting an exodus, the island is also seeing a few signs of a growing free market. People are selling items on the street, from bread, eggs, and other items, often via porch-front garage sales. As NPR noted, the private sector is the only part of the economy that is growing. Slowly, Cuba has allowed some privately owned hotels, restaurants, and businesses (Peralta, 2023).

US POLICY ON CUBA

Since he took power and for many decades, the US attempted to assassinate Fidel Castro. This is in violation of international law. Interestingly, it was not brought up by any of my interviewees. They hated Castro but I am not sure that any supported assassination efforts. The younger people did not seem aware of any of these things. The assassination attempts might sound laughable if they weren't an effort by one global superpower to remove the leader of another country. These efforts "were largely courtesy of the CIA, which reportedly devised no fewer than 638 plots to kill him, ranging from your typical poisoned handkerchief scheme to fungus-infected diving suits and exploding mollusks" (Fernandez, 2015).

Additionally, the US has many times attempted to wage war on Cuba. Reportedly top military officials drafted plans to kill innocent civilians in the US and to engage in terrorist acts that would be blamed on Cuba and enlist support for a war against the island. In the early 1960s, an effort with the Code name Operation Northwoods included the possible assassination of Cuban émigrés, sinking boats of Cuban refugees on the high seas, hijacking planes, blowing up a U.S. ship, and even orchestrating violent terrorism in U.S. cities. The plans were developed as ways to trick the American public and the international community into supporting a war to oust Cuba's then new leader, communist Fidel Castro." Further, they even plotted that "We could blow up a U.S. ship in Guantanamo Bay and blame Cuba," expressing that "casualty lists in U.S. newspapers would cause a helpful wave of national indignation. (ABC News, 2001).

In 1982, President Ronald Reagan added Cuba to the State Sponsor of Terror list. According to Venancio and Bare (2023), "The designation is intended for countries that have 'repeatedly provided support for acts of international terrorism,' but it is not imposed on the basis of human rights abuses, authoritarian backsliding, or military operations that lack an element of international terrorism." Cuba remained on that list until 2015, when President Obama lifted it, then was re-added by President Trump in 2021 and remained in 2024 under the Biden administration until the end of his term. Aside from the fact that the designation does not seem to fit Cuba, Venancio and Bare (2023) noted the many human costs as well. These are essentially the same as the human costs of the trade embargo. Being on the State Sponsor of Terror lists makes it more difficult to deliver humanitarian aid, which is much needed in Cuba. Banks, financial institutions, and corporations are hesitant to do business with Cuba, thereby further hurting the economy. It has a chilling effect on academic exchanges and travel.

In 1995, the US enacted a policy commonly referred to as "wet foot, dry foot." Many see this as one more Cuban privilege. As it sounds, the policy allows Cubans who touch US soil to stay in the country and get on the fast track to citizenship. If caught at sea, they were turned away. This privilege was not afforded to any other immigrant group. The threat that they could be sent back to Cuba if caught on the water was supposed to deter Cubans from making the trip and encourage them to immigrate through other channels, but it clearly did not. While there was much to worry about in traversing to the US by boat, Cubans basically did not have to worry about being undocumented. Guillermo Grenier, a Cuban American Sociology professor at Florida International University, explained, "Cubans have never been, and have never seen themselves, as 'illegals,' or even, particularly, as a minority group. They have never seen themselves as anything other than added value to this country. It's part of the Cuban exceptionalism narrative that is just as strong as the American exceptionalism narrative." President Obama ended the policy in 2017, much to the chagrin of many Cuban Americans (Florido, 2017).

One incident that highlights some of the challenges in how the US addresses Cuban immigrants was the case of Elian Gonzalez. In November 1999, Elizabeth Gonzalez attempted to bring her five-year-old son Elian to the US with her common law husband Lázaro Munero García and a dozen others on a small boat. Elizabeth died en route as did most of the others, as the rickety boat with a faulty engine got caught in a storm. One couple managed to get to shore, and young Elian was found on Thanksgiving Day, floating on an inner tube about five kilometers from the coast of Fort Lauderdale. Two fishermen found the boy and took him to the hospital. He was released the following day to his uncle Lazaro Gonzalez and other relatives living in the US. His father, Juan Miguel Gonzalez, still in Cuba, wanted him returned, as he had no idea Elizabeth had planned to leave with his son. On November 28, he filed a complaint with the UN to get attention to his plea for custody. One day later the US State Department recused itself from making a decision about custody of Elian, leaving it up to the state of Florida. Thus began a several month debacle, including a pre-dawn raid by armed federal agents to seize the boy from his relatives and return him to his father, who had made it to the US. This was all over national media, and the image of "Armed agents with tear gas and guns swarmed the Gonzalez family, who were unarmed," was not a good look (Swanson & Garcia, 2019). Two months and many court proceedings later, Elian and his father were finally back in Cuba (Abraham, 2015). More than just a fight over custody, the incident was a showdown between the two countries. He became a "symbol of both the exiles' unyielding opposition to the Castro regime and Havana's unyielding opposition to Washington" (Powell, 2022, p. 234).

Gigi Anders (2005) wrote about how she discussed the Elian case with her gringo boyfriend. She and her family did not want Elian returned to his father in Cuba, commenting that "Communists can't be good parents." She connected with the case, as her parents also fled Cuba so that she was not raised under the Castro regime. Her thoughts were indicative of many exiles, articulated in Spanglish, " I identified with him. My parents didn't want me to live in Cuba under Castro, either. They also took risks to get me from there when I was a tiny child. So, to see all of Elian's mom's effort and risk and even death come to noting for her son except a u-turn ticket back to Cuba after living it up here was just sadder than any words" (p. 142). This was the position held by most of the exile community. When Elian was returned to Cuba, Cuban Americans in Miami rioted and held a one-day work stoppage in Haileah. My interviewees actually did not bring up the case, to my surprise, but I subsequently asked David and he said most felt that he should stay here, as his mother risked her life for him. In all likelihood it was this case that swung the key Florida vote for Republican George W. Bush over Democrat Al Gore, as many considered the debacle the failure of Democrat Bill Clinton and of Democrats in general. As some have called it, the election was their *voto de castigo*, or punishment vote. Further, "By attempting to block Elian's return to his father, Cuban Americans put themselves starkly at odd with prevailing public opinion," and the entire affair made Miami look out-of-control (Powell, 2022, p. 234). Interestingly, Elian is now serving in Cuba's National Assembly.

The US continues to have a comprehensive embargo that was first authorized by President John F. Kennedy banned trade and financial transactions with Cuba unless licensed by the Treasury Department. This was an expansion of the previous administration's prohibitions on all trade to the island except food and medicine. Although the specifics changed over different administrations, the basics of the embargo remained the same and are, outside of a brief time President Obama lifted them, still in effect. There are very real economic effects of the trade embargo, as was noted in Chapter 2, but it is also a humanitarian disaster that has failed to accomplish anything but hurting the Cuban people. Oliver and Venancio (2022) make several recommendations, which include,

1. Suspending U.S. regulations that impede food, medicine, and other humanitarian assistance from reaching the Cuban people.
2. Removing all restrictions on family and non-family remittances.
3. Fully re-staffing the U.S. Embassy in Havana, with the necessary measures to ensure the safety of U.S. personnel and resuming consular services in Cuba.
4. Rolling back the Trump administration's measures that restrict travel to Cuba, since they limit mutually beneficial dialogue between the U.S. and Cuban people and make it more difficult for Cuban Americans to visit and reunite with family on the island, particularly for those with families outside of Havana (Para. 19).

President Obama was the first to seriously address the US and its failed policies with Cuba. He engaged in dialogue with Fidel Castro in December 2014, and they agreed to try to normalize relations between the two countries. This included establishing diplomatic relations, opening embassies in both countries, restored flights and mail service, and worked on initiatives to cooperate on health, education, agriculture, law enforcement, and more. In a 2016 speech in Cuba, President Obama thanked Castro for the warm welcome that he and his family received and commented, "I have come here to bury the last remnant of the Cold War in the Americas. (Applause.) I have come here to extend the hand of friendship to the Cuban people. (Applause.)." He explained why this was important: "What the United States was doing was not working. We have to have the courage to acknowledge that truth. A policy of isolation designed for the Cold War made little sense in the 21st century. The embargo was only hurting the Cuban people instead of helping them" (Office of the Press Secretary, 2016). Yet, as Eckstein (2022) noted, while the Obama administrated made some adjustments to Cuban privilege, it still afforded immigration status to Cubans and deported more than 1,500 Haitians and close to a half million other immigrants (Eckstein, 2022). In 2016 alone, more than 56,000 Cubans came to the US without authorization but due to Cuban privilege, after a brief detention they were admitted, given a variety of benefits, and faced no risk of deportation. This is in stark contrast to the more than 1,500 Haitians deported that year (Eckstein, 2022).

The Trump administration quickly undid all of the Obama-era advancements. It issued tougher sanctions on Cuba, restricting family remittances and travel and making it more difficult to get visas. There was a cap on remittances, prohibiting family members in the US from sending more than $1000 (£811) every three months. Trump cited human rights as his concern and denounced President Obama for trying to normalize relations (Holland, 2017). Yet, even as he deplored

Havana's human rights record, the Trump administration deported "unprecedented numbers back to one of the most insular and controlled societies on the planet" (Powell, 2022, p. 256).

President Biden lifted some of those, opening up travel with expanded flights to Havana, as well as permitting donations to non-family members (BBC News, 2022). The Biden administration issued a new parole policy in January 2023, requiring that potential migrants request a permit or parole online before arriving with the sponsorship of a relative of acquaintance already living in the U.S. This change applies to Cubans, Nicaraguans, and Haitians. The hope is that the program will reduce the number of migrants flooding through risky routes in Mexico. In the 2021–2022 fiscal year, border control had a record 224,000 encounters with Cuban migrants on the Mexico border. Border control stopped 29,878 Cuban migrants at the border in October 2022 alone, then 44,064 in November 2022. The policy also caps the number of migrants from these three countries as well as Venezuela to 30,000 per month an allows them to stay in the US for up to two months as long as they have a credible sponsor. Persons who try to reach the border without permission are to be detained and deported and will not be able to enter US territory, legally or otherwise, for five years. It does not specify if the number of migrants accepted from each of the four countries will be evenly split (Espinosa et al., 2022). At the time this book is in its final edits before publication, President Biden is expected to remove Cuba from the list of state sponsors of terror before he leaves office. President Trump reversed course shortly after taking office in 2025.

CONCLUSION

Although by no means exhaustive, my review of US-Cuba policy here and in other chapters reveals decades of disaster that did nothing to topple the Castro regimes (Fidel and then Raul) or to bring democracy to Cuba. I was surprised that my interviewees were generally unaware of these policies and how they have affected the Cuban people. As was discussed in Chapter 5, the idealization of Cuba pre-revolutionary seems to have left this family largely unconcerned about the island after the exiles left. I am hopeful that through the conversations I have had (as well as perhaps reading this book!), my interviewees will become more engaged in considering their homeland and in advocating for the Cuban people. For those interested in helping Cubans, we found that the easiest way to travel to Cuba is to do so with the Visa "Support for the Cuban People." This costs $100 and can be purchased at the airport so is super easy. But, rather than just a way to get to the island, we truly wanted to help. So, we researched what items are most needed and took an old suitcase filled with toiletries, diapers and baby items, Tylenol, non-perishable clothes and more. We left it there with our host, who promised to distribute to people in need in the community.

IMAGE 7.1.   David, Laura, and Daughter Anya in Matanzas, Cuba, Summer 2023

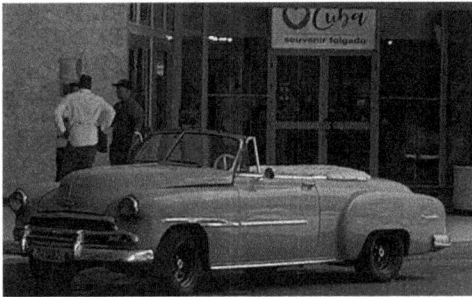

IMAGE 7.2.   One of the Many Amazing Cars in Cuba today.

REFERENCES

ABC News. (2001, April 30). *U.S. military wanted to provoke war with Cuba.* https://abc-news.go.com/US/story?id=92662&page=1

Abraham, D. (2015, May). *The Cuban Adjustment Act of 1966: Past and future.* Research Solutions. https://media.law.miami.edu/faculty-administration/pdf/david-abraham/cuban-adj-act.pdf

American Experience. (2005). *Cuban exiles in America.* PBS. https://www.pbs.org/wgbh/americanexperience/features/castro-cuban-exiles-america/

Anders, G. (2005). *Jubana! The awkwardly true and dazzling adventures of a Jewish Cubana Goddess.* HarperCollins.

BBC News. (2022, May 17). *US agrees to ease Trump-era sanctions on Cuba.* https://www.bbc.com/news/world-europe-61473884

Behar, R. (Ed.). (1995). *Bridges to Cuba.* University of Michigan Press.

Eckstein, S. (2009). *The immigrant divide: How Cubans changes the US and their homeland.* Routledge.

Eckstein, S. (2022). *Cuban privilege: The making of immigrant inequality in America.* Cambridge University Press.

Espinos, M., Venancio, M., & Omodt, N. (2022, December 16). *U.S.-Cuba relations: The old, the new, and what should come next.* WOLA. https://www.wola.org/analysis/us-cuba-relations-old-new-should-come-next/

Fernandez, B. (2015, February 7). *Killing Fidel.* Al Jazeera. https://www.aljazeera.com/opinions/2015/2/7/killing-fidel

Filosa, G. (2022, December 14). *Surge in Cuban migrants landing in the Keys in homemade boats.* WLRN. https://www.wlrn.org/immigration/2022-12-14/surge-in-cuban-migrants-landing-in-the-keys-in-homemade-boats

Florido, A. (2017, January 15). End of "wet-foot, dry-foot" means Cubans can join ranks of "undocumented." NPR. https://www.npr.org/sections/codeswitch/2017/01/15/509895837/end-of-wet-foot-dry-foot-means-cubans-can-join-ranks-of-the-undocumented

Goodhue, D. (2023, January 1). Multiple migrant landings mark the start of 2034 in the Florida Keys. *Miami Herald.* https://www.miamiherald.com/news/local/community/florida-keys/article270636822.html

Holland, S. (2017, June 16). *Trump rolls back parts of what he calls "terrible" Obama Cuba policy.* Reuters. https://www.reuters.com/article/world/trump-rolls-back-parts-of-what-he-calls-terrible-obama-cuba-policy-idUSKBN1971NW/

Kaplan, D. (2000). A Jewish renaissance in Castro's Cuba. *Judaism: A Quarterly Journal of Jewish Life and Thought, 49*(2), 218–236.

Office of the Press Secretary. (2016, March 22). *Remarks by President Obama to the Cuban people.* https://obamawhitehouse.archives.gov/the-press-office/2016/03/22/remarks-president-obama-people-Cuba

Oliver, I., & Venancio, M. (2022, February 4). U*nderstanding the failure of the U.S. embargo on Cuba.* WOLA. https://www.wola.org/analysis/understanding-failure-of-us-cuba-embargo/

Peralta, A. (2023, September 28). *Cuba's worst economic crisis in decades forces people to get creative to survive.* NPR. https://www.npr.org/2023/09/28/1202264839/cuba-s-worst-economic-crisis-in-decades-forces-people-to-get-creative-to-survive

Powell, D. (2022). *Ninety miles and a lifetime away: Memories of early Cuban exiles.* University Press of Florida.

Reuters in Havana. (2023, September 28). Cuban officials warn of increased blackouts due to fuel shortages. *The Guardian.* https://www.theguardian.com/world/2023/sep/28/cuba-power-blackouts-fuel-shortage

Risech, F. (1995). Political and cultural cross-dressing: Negotiating a second generation Cuban-American identity. In Behar, R. (Ed.), *Bridges to Cuba* (pp. 57–71). University of Michigan Press.

Stephens, A. (2021). Making migrants "criminal": The Mariel boatlift, Miami, and U.S. immigration policy in the 1980s. *Anthurian Caribbean Studies Journal.* https://anthurium.miami.edu/articles/10.33596/anth.439#welcome-to-miami

Swanson, J., & Garcia, A. (2019, November 11). *Why the Elian Gonzalez case resonates 20 years later.* Vox. https://www.vox.com/the-highlight/2019/11/4/20938885/miami-cuba-elian-gonzalez-castro

Torres, N., & Ortiz-Blanes, S. (2023, January 4). Desperation is driving latest surge of Cuban rafters arriving in the Florida Keys. *Tampa Bay Times.* https://www.tampabay.com/news/florida-politics/2023/01/04/desperation-is-driving-latest-surge-cuban-rafters-arriving-florida-keys/

U.S. Department of Defense. (2020, July 2). *The "other" boatlift: Camarioca, Cuba, 1965.* https://media.defense.gov/2020/Jul/02/2002356759/-1/-1/0/CAMARIOCA1965.PDF

Venancio, M., & Bare, A. (2023). *The human cost of Cuba's inclusion on the State Sponsor of Terrorism list.* Washington Office on Latin America. https://www.wola.org/analysis/human-cost-cuba-state-sponsor-of-terrorism-list/

CONCLUSION

I have been honored to be able to engage in this research, to learn about the Jew-bans and their trajectory, and even to share some things with the family. As I noted in the Introduction, I do not profess to be an expert on Cuba, Judaism, or Jewbans. I am still a novice, for sure. But here, I am summarizing what I see as some of the key takeaways I have identified, including areas for additional research. I also offer implications for peace educators.

TAKEAWAYS

First, the prevailing narrative amongst this family, and it seems among other Jew-ban families I read about, is that Cuba pre-revolution was a paradise and that all ended when Castro came to power. This view is not inaccurate, but it also is not complete. I believe that it has, however, created a victimization narrative that was reinforced by US policy that gave Cuban exiles the most generous benefits ever (and to this day) afforded to any immigrant group. "What is the ethos of the exile experience for us? The ethos is the sense of loss, the mythology of exile, which is very beautiful. You're pure because you left. But more than anything else is a sense of honor and achievement. You have to achieve. Because you lost all this, you are called on to be better than anybody else. You cannot be second best. We had that inbred: You have to show people that you came from a great family in

Shiksa Speaks: A White, Non-Jew's Understanding of the
Cuban Jewish Diaspora and Its Legacy, 123–127.
Copyright © 2025 *Laura Finley*
Published under exclusive licence by Emerald Publishing Limited
HB: 978-1-83708-494-4, PB: 978-1-83708-495-1, ePDF: 978-1-83708-496-8

a great country that was stolen from you. You have to do great things (Powell, 2022, p. 236).

Second, the success of the Jewbans and this family specifically is undeniable and incredibly admirable. As the daughter of an immigrant (my mother from England) and someone whose heritage includes Irish immigrants on both sides, I know that financial success of the scope and extent that is true with the Jewbans is generally not true of other groups. As noted, the family narrative is that it is due to work ethic, risk-taking, and resilience, all of which are true. However, compared to other immigrant groups these families started with more resources and support, were more educated so better able to advance, and came from industries that were easier to achieve financial success. Irish immigrants, for example, tended to work in factories or farms, neither of which tend to be lucrative nor offer an easy pathway to advancement.

Third, it struck me that because many exiles feel themselves to be uniquely victimized as especially the Jewbans with the double diaspora, their response is to largely freeze time and not concern themselves with Cuba today. This they passed on, for the most part, to their children and grandchildren. Thus, no one was particularly interested in or knowledgeable about Cuba today, outside of Ester, Marcos, and David. Most are not very familiar with Cuban history, either, as that was not taught. Hence why these interviewees did not go to celebrations of Marti, monuments to him, or other historical sites. Their Cubanness is, as was discussed, manifests pretty much in language, food, and music.

Fourth, what I learned about the Cuban exiles and the Jewbans across generations contrasts fairly starkly with my own family's experience and with that of most other immigrant groups. For one, my mother immigrated from England in 1970, after she and my father met while he was serving there in the Air Force. Her move was voluntary, as she wanted to live with her husband in Michigan. While the exiles did choose to move to the US, their decision was under significantly different circumstances. Additionally, my mother was quite poor in England, as was my dad and his family in Michigan. To illustrate: he proposed a year before they wed but had to return to Michigan because of the flight the Air Force arranged due to his end of service. Neither of them had telephones in their homes so they had to write each other letters throughout the year, and they talked once on a pay phone. He had to mail her an engagement ring, which she had to pay taxes on! They definitely did not have maids or some of the other things that are typical of a middle-class life and that many of the exiles had in Cuba. While my newlywed parents had my dad's parents nearby in Michigan, they also had very little so were unable to provide the kind of assistance that family offered to Lilia and Jack. As well, my dad was working as a mechanic and my mom had done secretarial work in England. Neither had any higher education nor had experience in business or starting businesses, as did some of the members of this family. One thing that was similar was culture shock in regard to weather and expectations.

As was noted in Chapter 6, Cubans were and, to a lesser degree, still are more easily able to immigrate to the US than other groups. They were afforded benefits that helped them get acclimated that contributed to their success. Eckstein (2009, 2022) documented the dramatic difference between how Cuban and Haitian immigrants have been treated. Today, the US is grappling with a complex mess in its immigration policy and border control. Powell (2022) noted the many parallels between the early Cuban refugees and today's immigration debates over what to do with refugee children, family reunification, pathways to citizenship, government assistance to immigrants and more. He noted, "These issues about contemporary refugees resonate with Cuban Americans. Or should" (p. 254). My interviewees, on the whole, did not seem to see such parallels.

IMPLICATIONS FOR PEACE EDUCATORS

One thing peace educators can do is advocate for more comprehensive teaching of Cuban history in K–12 schools as well as in higher education. I know that I am not alone in realizing that my schooling about Cuba and its important and unique relationship to the US was terrifically inadequate. Critiquing colonialism and imperialism is often part of peace studies. The imperialist nature of the United States' involvement in the history is critical in understanding how the revolution took shape and the conditions in Cuba today. In particular, peace educators can share with students the failed Cold War-era approaches the US used to try to destabilize Cuba and overthrow Castro. That the US many times attempted to assassinate a country's leader is abominable and students should know that while the US criticizes Cuba for its human rights record, ours on the island is not too stellar. As our tour guide Ronald expressed to us, the US spreads misinformation about Cuba and always has. Peace educators can help to correct these misconceptions.

Second, peace educators teaching about immigration and acclimation can point to the successes of the Jewbans and the many factors that influenced it. This could include teaching about the differences in immigration policy between Cubans and other groups. Students can assess the rationale for these differences, how they have affected different groups, and whether similar benefits that were afforded to the Cubans should be provided to other immigrants, as Powell (2022) and Eckstein (2022) suggested. Comparing the reception of other groups who are definitely refugees to that of exile Cubans could help students develop understanding, empathy, and encourage them to advocate for more humane immigration policy. Like Eckstein (2022), I am hopeful that this book might help readers see how immigration policy can be more equitable and also how the United States has and can continue to benefit from immigrants.

Third, peace educators can use this research to highlight the importance of narrative in developing identity. As Chapter 3 showed, the double diaspora resulted in Jewban exiles more likely identifying as Jewish than Cuban, which they have passed along to their family. Further, narrative has shaped this family's consideration of Cuba, its engagement in politics, and its connections (and general lack thereof) of Cuban waves that arrived later than they did.

Additional research to compare the exiles experience with that of persons who arrived as part of Operation Pedro Pan would be interesting (and is in the works!). While I was able to interview Marcos who came via Pedro Pan, I have much to learn about their stories, experiences, reception in the US, and successes. Powell (2022) does capture many of these stories, but further research could elaborate on similarities and differences between these groups that arrived in the US around the same time but in different fashion and with different supports.

Another line of inquiry would be to interview Jewbans living in areas outside of South Florida and even the US. While I interviewed several people who currently reside in other locations, they all spent their childhood and teen years in South Florida and are still quite connected to it via family ties. The experience of Jewbans who remained in New York or New Orleans, for instance, might be quite different. As Eckstein (2022) noted, another advantage the exiles had was that they arrived in Miami at just the right time. The city was on the cusp of dramatic expansion and the exiles helped to build and enhance that. The federal and state benefits given to Cubans were an important part of that growth. Similarly, Jewbans who emigrated to Israel likely had a significantly different experience that would be interesting to compare and contrast.

IMAGE 8.1.
Jack Bekerman

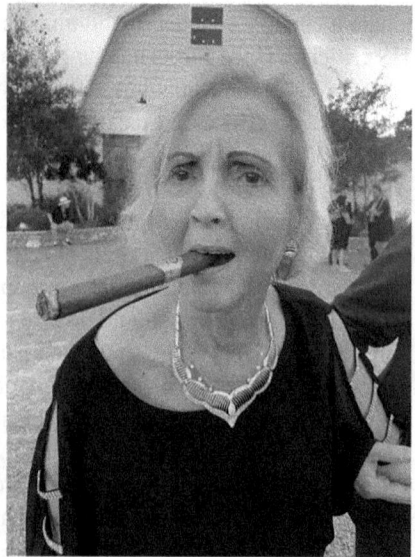

IMAGE 8.2.
"Bad Ass" Lilia Bekerman

In sum, I am deeply grateful to have been able to conduct this research, both academically and personally. I hope that what I have written sheds some light on the experience and successes of the Jewbans. I also hope that it is an appropriate and loving tribute to Jack Bekerman, may he rest in peace, and to my beautiful mother-in-law, Lilia. She has a wonderful, loving personality and a great sense of humor. One of my favorite stories is when I referred to her in a Facebook post as a "bad ass," meaning it as a term of endearment. She was unfamiliar with the term and asked Perry why I said she had a "big ass!" Now that she knows what bad ass means, we joke about it and even got her a necklace that says the term. May she forever remain spicy!

REFERENCES

Eckstein, S. (2009). *The immigrant divide: How Cuban Americans changed the U.S. and their homeland.* Routledge.

Eckstein, S. (2022). *Cuban privilege: The making of immigrant inequality in America.* Cambridge University Press.

Powell, D. (2022). *Ninety miles and a lifetime away: Memories of early Cuban exiles.* University of Florida Press.

AUTHOR BIOGRAPHY

Laura Finley, Ph.D. is Professor of Sociology & Criminology at Barry University in Miami Shores, Florida. She is author, co-author or editor of 35 books and dozens of peer-reviewed journal articles and book chapters. Finley is also a syndicated columnist with *PeaceVoice*. She is a frequent presenter at local, state, and national conferences as well. In addition, Dr. Finley is Board Vice-President for The Humanity Project and a Board member with Floridians for Alternatives to the Death Penalty.

www.ingramcontent.com/pod-product-compliance
Lightning Source LLC
Chambersburg PA
CBHW070347270326
41926CB00017B/4030